ArtScroll Series®

Rabbi Nosson Scherman / Rabbi Meir Zlotowitz
General Editors

Life

Published by
Mesorah Publications, ltd

Is Now

Rabbi Zelig Pliskin

FIRST EDITION
First Impression ... August 2009

Published and Distributed by
MESORAH PUBLICATIONS, LTD.
4401 Second Avenue / Brooklyn, N.Y 11232

Distributed in Europe by
LEHMANNS
Unit E, Viking Business Park
Rolling Mill Road
Jarow, Tyne & Wear, NE32 3DP
England

Distributed in Australia and New Zealand
by **GOLDS WORLDS OF JUDAICA**
3-13 William Street
Balaclava, Melbourne 3183
Victoria, Australia

Distributed in Israel by
SIFRIATI / A. GITLER — BOOKS
6 Hayarkon Street
Bnei Brak 51127

Distributed in South Africa by
KOLLEL BOOKSHOP
Ivy Common
105 William Road
Norwood 2192, Johannesburg, South Africa

ARTSCROLL SERIES®
LIFE IS NOW
© Copyright 2009, by MESORAH PUBLICATIONS, Ltd.
4401 Second Avenue / Brooklyn, N.Y. 11232 / (718) 921-9000 / www.artscroll.com

---

ALL RIGHTS RESERVED
The text, prefatory and associated textual contents and introductions
— including the typographic layout, cover artwork and ornamental graphics —
have been designed, edited and revised as to content, form and style.

No part of this book may be reproduced
IN ANY FORM, PHOTOCOPYING, OR COMPUTER RETRIEVAL SYSTEMS
— even for personal use without written permission from
the copyright holder, Mesorah Publications Ltd.
except by a reviewer who wishes to quote brief passages
in connection with a review written for inclusion in magazines or newspapers.

THE RIGHTS OF THE COPYRIGHT HOLDER WILL BE STRICTLY ENFORCED.

ISBN 10: 1-4226-0921-9 / ISBN 13: 978-1-4226-0921-7

Typography by CompuScribe at ArtScroll Studios, Ltd.
Printed in Canada
Bound by Sefercraft, Quality Bookbinders, Ltd., Brooklyn N.Y. 11232

*I dedicate this book to the memory
of a great person who had a
major impact on my life*

Rabbi Noah Weinberg זצ״ל

In memory of

My Father ע״ה
and My Mother ע״ה

*Now in the present
I am more grateful than ever before.
I owe them everything.*

In memory of my father-in-law

Rabbi Simcha Weissman זצ״ל

*I am forever grateful for his constant kindness
and dedication to raising a Torah family.
His joy and sacrifice for Torah and mitzvos
served as an inspiration to all who knew him.*

Table of Contents

	Acknowledgments	11
	Introduction	13
1.	The Essence of Life: Reality is Now	17
2.	Choosing Wisely on Your Life's Journey	21
3.	You Were Blessed on the Day You Were Born	24
4.	Today Is a New Day and You Can Begin a New Day at Any Time During the Day	27
5.	Now, What Does the Almighty Want from Me?	31
6.	Today is the Greatest Day of Your Life	33
7.	The Book of Your Life Is Made Up of a Multitude of Short Stories	36
8.	Accept What You Feel Now and You Will Be Open to Better Feelings in a Moment	39
9.	What Would Be the Best State for Now?	42
10.	Act Now the Way You Wish to Be	46
11.	"What Can I Do Now to Move Forward on My Priority Goals?"	49
12.	To Concentrate, Focus Your Total Attention on What You Are Doing Now	52
13.	See And Hear What You Can See And Hear Right Now	55
14.	Curiosity Each Day: "What Will Be Today's Highlights?"	57
15.	Regardless of Your Past Self-Image, Right Now You Can See Yourself in a Better Light	60

16. Every Encounter with Another Person Happens in the Here and Now	64
17. Everything Is Perfect Right Now	68
18. Having Enough for Today Gives You an Abundant Life Today	70
19. Everything Before Now Is Your Present Past: Elevate It in Your Mind	73
20. "Right Now I Am Alive, and I Release All Stress and Tension."	76
21. Joy Made Easy: The Nine Principles for Happiness and Joy for Individuals and Groups	80
22. Focusing on What's Wrong and What's Missing	83
23. The Art and Skill of Creating More Moments of Joy	86
24. The Special Word that Creates Joy	89
25. Focusing on Joy is the Key to Being More Joyful	93
26. Your Creator Gave You an Endorphin Factory	96
27. Joy Is Created and Stored in Your Brain	99
28. Send Joyful Energy to Your Brain, Heart, Lungs, Throat, Tongue, etc.	102
29. The Most Joyful Feeling in the World	105
30. If I Were a Master of Joy, How Would I Speak and Act Now?	107
31. What a Group of 2-Year-Olds Taught Me About Joy	110
32. Persist to Master Joy	113
33. The Self-talk of Joy	116
34. Determination to Be Joyful Today Will Enable You to Create a More Joyful Day	119
35. You Are Alive! Therefore You Have a Reason to Be Joyful	122
36. Count Joyfully	125
37. "I Am Joyfully Grateful for Each and Every Breath."	127
38. Keep a Joy Journal	130
39. What Stops You from Creating More Joyful Moments?	132
40. Your Moments of Joy Are Unique to You	136

41. "Have a Joyful Day!"	139
42. Take a Joy Walk	141
43. Transform Frustration into Joy	143
44. Bake "Joy Cookies"	146
45. Joy for Eating Wisely and Joy for Refraining from Eating Unwisely	148
46. Bless 18 People Each Day to Be Joyful	151
47. Joyful Dreams	153
48. Reviving Downhearted Spirits	156
49. Life Is Now: Creating Moments of Kindness	160
50. Life Is Now: Creating Moments of Courage	162
51. Life Is Now: Creating Moments of Serenity	166
52. When You Think of Your Past, Think: "Joy!"	170
53. Obsessing About What Might Go Wrong in the Future	174
54. "How Can I Be Certain that I Will Never Think Another Negative Thought?"	177
55. The "4 for Self-Creation" Program	180
56. The Four-finger Button Technique for Joy, Courage, Love, and Serenity	186
57. "The Joy, Courage, Love, and Serenity Chant"	190
58. The Life-transforming Personal Program	193
59. See, Hear, and Feel "Joy, Courage, Kindness, and Serenity" in the Past, Present, and Future	196
60. Upgrading Your Identity and Learning From Others	200
61. Nine-directions Mental Conditioning: Joy, Courage, Loving-kindness, and Serenity	203
62. You Write Your Script Every Time You Speak	205
63. Use Your Imagination Wisely	208
64. I Can Do Anything that is Not Impossible for Me to Do	211
65. "Oheiv Es HaMakom …" Meditation	214
66. Lack of Self-love Causes a Deficiency of "Love for the Almighty, and Love for People"	217
67. "Inner Joy" Meditation	221

68. The "I Radiate Joy and Love!" Exercise	224
69. Awesome Joy	226
70. Look in a Mirror and Say to Yourself, "Awesome Joy"	230
71. It's Going to Become Easier and Easier for Me to …	233
72. Find the Humor	235
73. The Power of "Enough is Enough"	237
74. Don't Sell Yourself Short	240
75. Setbacks and Disappointments Can Develop Your Character	244
76. Envy: the Art and Science of Feeling Bad Because Someone Else Feels Good	247
77. Choose Joy and Love to Melt Anger	250
78. Life Is Now: Creating a Moment of … Whatever You Want to Create Now	253
79. ABC: Spell for Joy and Upgrading Your Mind	259
80. A Tourist's Guide for Today on Our Planet	266
81. A Tale of Two Towns: What is the Difference?	270
82. Joy: "It's Up to Me!"	272

Acknowledgments

I am grateful to the Almighty for His constant kindness. I pray that this book be a source of inspiration and happiness for many.

I am grateful to the entire ArtScroll staff for all they have done to publish this book and my previous ArtScroll books. I am especially grateful to Reb Shmuel Blitz, Reb Avrohom Biderman, and Reb Mendy Herzberg.

I am once again grateful to Mrs. Tova Ovits for her masterful editing. I greatly appreciate her professionalism.

I am grateful to Mrs. Sarah Shapiro for her insightful and cogent comments on the manuscript. Her insight was very helpful.

I am grateful to the late Rosh Hayeshiva of Aish Hatorah, Rabbi Noah Weinberg, of blessed memory. I have gained greatly from him in many ways.

I am grateful to my dear friend Rabbi Kalman Packouz for his friendship and encouragement. He is a world-class expert on reframing. I have gained a lot from his valuable insights.

I am grateful to all those who attended classes at the Jerusalem Joy Club. Their comments and questions were extremely helpful.

I express my gratitude to my dear friend Lionel Ketchian, founder of The Happiness Club (happinessclub.com). In our mastermind dialogue we conceived of the creation of 1000 happiness/joy clubs around the world.

Introduction

I wish that I would have read this book 50 years ago. The ideas presented here are not new. But as we get older, we understand concepts differently. Somehow, ideas that we heard long ago seem new to us. Had I read this book 50 years ago and reread it now, I would understand new ways to improve my life. We all live, breathe, and make all our choices in the present. As you read this book right now, you are choosing what to think, say, and do in reference to reading this book. I pray that if this is your first time reading it, you will choose to read the entire book. If you have already read it before, I pray that you will continue to gain by reading it.

Life is an ongoing process. You started your life when you were born, and you have an entire lifetime of "present moments" to fulfill your mission in this world. I hope this book will serve as a guide for improving many present moments in your life.

We need to wisely balance our thinking about the past, present, and future. We have much to learn from our own life's history. We will gain much from planning and preparing for the future.

Nevertheless, all the choices we make about what to think, say, and do are made now, in the present.

You are in the present when you read this book. And you will be in the present whenever you choose to apply what you know. The past is just the history of how you thought about yourself and your life.

The way you think about yourself and your life in any present moment is the key to how you actually experience it. You are extremely fortunate: The fact that you understand these words means that you are alive and your mind is working.

In the first passage in the last chapter of *Pirkei Avos*, Rabbi Meir tells us that everyone who studies Torah with pure motivation will merit many things. Among the long list is: "Love for Hashem and love for people, bringing joy to Hashem and joy to people."

Only with a personal experience of inner joy will we be able to achieve this level. Therefore, joy is a major focus of this book. When you are authentically joyful, you will find it easier to create more moments of courage, love for Hashem and other people, inner peace and serenity, and many other positive ways of being.

Giving a "Joy Workshop" to a group of 2-year-olds has shown me how easy it is to teach young children to be joyful. (I will describe this experience later in the book.) As we grow older, we easily learn how to *not* be joyful. The ideas you read in this book will make it easier for you to be more joyful more often.

This book contains nine principles for mastering happiness and joy, which appeared in *Conversations with Yourself*. These principles have proven highly beneficial for individuals and groups. Teachers of happiness will be able to elaborate on these themes.

This book also contains a summary of my self-development workshop: "Four for Self-Creation." The four refers to: Self-talk, Self-image, Goals, and Traits-States. There are also tools for easy access to the 4 traits-states that will make the biggest difference in your life: Joy, Courage, Love ("I love You, Hashem *Yisbarach*") and Serenity. As will be elaborated in the chapter "The Four for Self-Creation Program," traits are a pattern of our thoughts, words, and actions while states are moment-by-moment experiences.

Every individual will have unique challenges with each of these four qualities. This book is not about always being joyful, courageous, loving, kind, and serene. Rather, it has a more modest goal: to create more moments of each positive quality.

As a "joy coach and self-image builder," I teach my students new ways of thinking and acting. These methods increase their moments of joy and their general attitudes toward themselves and their lives.

There is a major difference between gaining knowledge and mastering a skill. People who read this book already know that they live in the present moment. Everyone knows the past is over and the future has not happened yet. Nevertheless, some people spend too much time rehashing the past. Others spend too much time worrying about the future. Some people needlessly limit themselves by not planning sufficiently for creating a better future; they narrowly and excessively focus on the present. Learning a healthy and wise balance of past, present, and future is a skill that we need to learn and can learn by increasing our knowledge and experience.

The positive qualities of Joy, Courage, Love (for the Creator, for kindness, and for other people), and Serenity are valuable qualities. It takes skill to implement them in our daily lives. This book should make it easier for you to keep developing these skills.

May you benefit from the ideas and techniques shared on these pages. I hope you will benefit so much that you will teach others what you have learned.

The essence of life: reality is now

In 1964, I read a poem that moved me greatly. It was written by the late Rabbi Eliyahu Eliezer Dessler in Hebrew, and was published in the third volume of his classic works *Michtav MeEliyahu*. Here is an English translation:

"The past is only memories. The future is but illusory hopes.
Focus on the present.
For that is where your life really is.
And it consists only of tests."
(Rabbi E.E. Dessler - Michtav MeEliyahu, vol. 3, p. 306)

I memorized the poem and have repeated it frequently over the years. It is profound. This short poem sums up one of the most important lessons we all need to live our lives to the fullest.

I first read this poem 45 years ago. I recently reflected on how understanding this poem could have saved so many people from much distress and suffering.

Much distress comes from needlessly thinking about past comments people thoughtlessly made. Much distress comes from being obsessed about past mistakes and errors, instead of learning from them and internalizing the wisdom gained.

Much distress comes from worrying about potential suffering that doesn't happen. Or, if the worrisome event actually takes place, it is much easier to handle than expected. Or the trouble causes many beneficial effects. If we could see the entire big picture instead of worrying about it, we would have smiled and appreciated what the Almighty sent our way.

Past experiences have shaped our lives and who we are. What we have already thought, said, and done in the past has created who we are now. Our past has a tremendous impact on our lives.

But since everything that has happened in the past has already happened, we can only make positive choices of what we plan, say, and do in the present. We can't change the past, but we can change the future.

Memories are valuable. Not remembering the past is one of the greatest handicaps a person can have. But being hampered and limited by the past is also a serious handicap. The greater our ability to master focusing on what we can think, say, and do now in the present, the more we will be able to transcend limitations of the past.

We need to plan for the future. We need the wisdom to realize the future results of what we say and do. It's possible to imagine how great everything will turn out. But imagination is not reality: We can't possibly know what will actually be in the future.

Reality is in the here and now. We live each moment of each day "now, in the present." Now we think any of the thoughts that we choose to think. Now we choose to say or not to say something. Now we decide what we will do or not do at any given moment.

What is the essence of each moment of life? It is Divinely orchestrated tests and challenges. Rabbi Dessler's poem is based on the first chapter of the classic *mussar* book, *Mesilas Yesharim*. There we read that everything is a test to help us elevate ourselves. Wealth is a test. Poverty is a test. When all is going well and we experience tranquility, that is a test. And when we are faced with difficult life challenges, they are a test as well.

When you are well prepared for a test and know that you are skilled, that you are able to do great work, you actually enjoy the tests that you take. They don't make you anxious or nervous. You feel an inner pleasure in knowing that you are passing the test.

Sometimes you know that a test is going to be difficult. But if the potential benefits of doing well on the test are magnificent, you mentally and physically prepare in every way you can to excel on the test. You devote all your time and energy to build up your skills and talents. You celebrate each bit of progress and improvement.

Preparing to master the challenges we face gives our life purpose and meaning. Actually doing well is a source of great joy. Those who realize that life is for growing and developing from each and every challenge, each day of our lives, live a life of joy.

> *Someone complained to me, "My life is full of one disappointment after another. I feel frustrated and upset when I think about all the things that haven't worked. When I think about my future, I don't expect that things will get much better. I feel simply awful most of the time. My life is dull and empty. I know that nothing is seriously wrong with my life. But overall I'm far from experiencing the joy and enthusiasm that I was always hoping for."*
>
> *"You're not alone," I told him. "But from what you told me about your life, you are only one attitude away from totally transforming your life.*
>
> *"You have experienced many disappointments in the past. The problem is that you relive them over and over again. The more you focus on those past disappointments, the more they color your life.*
>
> *"It's like you have an autobiography called, 'My Life Until Now.' You don't like what you are reading, yet you keep reading the same disappointing chapters over and over again, and you're skipping the happy chapters. That's not a very intelligent way to spend one's time.*
>
> *"In reality, you have much to be grateful for about the past. Moreover, you did accomplish much more than you are*

The Essence of Life: Reality Is Now

now giving yourself credit for. But it would be much wiser to keep your major focus on the present. Frustration comes from comparing what is to what you feel ought to be. When you make wise choices in the present and spend less time focusing on the past, much of your frustration will disappear.

"What you focus on expands. Your life challenge is to appreciate all that you can appreciate about the present. Your life challenge is to experience more joy in your present prayers and Torah study. Your life challenge is how to become a kinder more compassionate person and to experience more joy for the good that you do while you are doing it. Your life challenge is to constantly develop your character traits in the present.

"When you increase your level of understanding that every moment of your life is a challenge to choose wiser thoughts, words, and actions, you will experience more meaning and purpose each and every day. Every day is significant. Every day is valuable. Every day you can grow and develop yourself from that day's challenges."

After a week, I received feedback: "I'm amazed. This one change of focus can make such a major difference! I feel like I am living in a totally different world. The overriding frustration has been replaced by an excitement for life. Each day, I look forward to the good I can do that day. I don't need to wait for the long-term results to realize that each day I am doing something meaningful."

Choosing wisely on your life's journey

You make your life journey more meaningful and joyful when you choose wisely in the here and now. It's always "now." And as long as you are alive, you are still on your life's journey.

Every step of the way, you have the memories of every great and joyful moment of your life. In your brain's great archives, you have memories of everything positive from any time in your life.

In your brain you have all the important knowledge and wisdom that you have ever heard and read. In your brain you have every story about every great person that you either read or heard about at any time in your life. Even if you don't consciously remember those stories, they are stored in your subconscious mind. All you need to do is consciously focus on those main messages of those stories now.

Your mind and soul can choose to think, speak, and act wisely and meaningfully wherever you are at any given time. You live your entire life one moment at a time. You only need to choose to think one wise thought at a time. You only need to choose to say one positive sentence (or word) at a time. You only need to choose one meaningful action at a time. These all add up.

Don't waste an excessive amount of time on regrets about the past. Those who do then miss out on making more constructive present moments. Don't waste an excessive amount of time worrying about the future. Those who do then miss out on the best and wisest thoughts and actions right here and now.

Keep climbing and elevating your self. Keep connecting with our Father, our King, Creator and Sustainer of the universe. Keep doing good in this world. Keep doing acts of kindness. Keep gaining more wisdom. Keep up the efforts of being the best you that you can be.

Your entire life journey will be more elevated when you continue developing your sense of identity and self-image. Your self-image has already changed: You began as a helpless infant, yet every year you accumulated more knowledge and life experiences than the year before.

Your present sense of identity depends upon how you see yourself right now. Your moods will change frequently. Sometimes you will feel joyful and sometimes you won't. Sometimes you will be calm and serene and sometime you won't. But your soul, which is your essence, is always pure and sacred. Identify with your eternal soul and see the major difference this will make on the rest of your journey through life.

Right now you are in the middle of your life's journey. We only complete our journey with our last breath. Every other breath gives us opportunities for more elevating thoughts, words, and actions. Keep choosing wisely.

> *The story that goes here is the ongoing story of your life. You are writing it with your thoughts, words, and actions. What will it consist of? Only you can choose.*
>
> *I have a suggestion for you: Make it a habit each and every*

day to write down a positive story about yourself. Describe something positive you said or did as if you were writing a biography about someone else. For example, if you said a kind word to someone, you can describe your act of kindness in glowing terms. You can write about the potential benefits of that kindness.

I am not referring to boasting about yourself. Rather, view it as a record of at least one positive thing you did each and every day. You are the only person you intend to impress when you later read the recorded actions.

Stories that you wrote about your own strengths and positive actions are the most inspiring stories you can read when you are facing challenging times. And if one day, your grandchildren or great-grandchildren read them and are inspired … (That's an inspiring thought to think.)

You were blessed on the day you were born

I magine that an amazing messenger from your Creator blessed you on the day you were born.

"Welcome to this planet, little one. You are starting out on your life mission. I want you to constantly remember that you are created in the Creator's image and you are His child. He has created this world for your benefit and for you to have a place to grow and develop your character.

"You will live your life one moment at a time. I bless you to appreciate and be grateful for life with every breath that you breathe. You will need to learn many things to make the most of your stay on Earth. I want to help you get off to a good start. So I bless you with four qualities. These four qualities will upgrade your self-talk when you learn how to speak.

"I bless you with joy. Whenever you say a blessing or pray or study Torah, do so with joy. Joy will make every spiritual word and action more elevated.

"I bless you with courage. Have the courage to fulfill your life's mission. Don't needlessly limit yourself with fear. I bless you to experience joy every time you do something you might fear.

"I bless you with love, love for your Creator and love for being kind to other people. Each word and act of kindness is another opportunity to experience more joy.

"I bless you with serenity. That will give you an inner calm and a clear mind to be able to think wisely and creatively.

"You will forget that you received this blessing. But this blessing will always be accessible whenever you wish to make it come true.

"These four qualities are skills that you can continue to master. Every thought, word, and action consistent with these qualities will enable them to get stronger and stronger.

"Every challenge that you experience is another opportunity to develop your character."

The very fact that you are reading this now is an expression of the blessing that you received on day one. Once read, these words are embedded in your brain and will have a quiet impact on your life.

I bless you that you enjoy your stay on this planet.

> *Someone who read this blessing gave me feedback. He exclaimed, "Wow!! As I read this, it immediately made me realize that every positive thing I hear and read is a positive message from my Creator.*
>
> *"I used to say to myself, 'I can't always be happy. Sometimes I experience courage and sometimes I don't. So I'm not really courageous. I would love to love the Creator, but that's a high level that I'm really far from. I feel stressed a lot of the time, and I'm far from serene. But after reading this, I started picturing how it would help to realize that a messenger from my Creator is blessing me right now with these qualities."*
>
> *A week later he added, "Since I realized that the Creator*

created me to live with these valuable qualities, it made it much easier to experience them on a practical, daily level. I look forward to the many benefits I will continue gaining from now on."

Today is a new day and you can begin a new day at any time during the day

When you wake up in the morning, the rest of your life begins again. How will you act on the momentous occasion of a new beginning? What would enable you to live today fully alive and energized?

When we wake up in the morning, we are off to the start of a new day. We start off each morning with an expression of gratitude to the Source of our life for giving us the gift of life today. A question that will enhance your life is: "How can I utilize this magnificent gift in the best possible way for today?"

You will live this entire day moment by moment, in the mental and emotional state of that moment. These states will fluctuate throughout the day. You will have moments of being more "up" and moments of not being so happy. Positive traits and states have names that you can call upon to access them in the best way you can, for now.

Four of the qualities that will benefit you greatly are: Joy, Courage, Love (for Hashem and other people), and Serenity (peace of mind and a state of well-being). Resolve to make these qualities the background of how you think, feel, speak, and act today.

Joy might not always be appropriate in a given situation or circumstance, but love for Hashem always is. And so is serenity, which is conducive for clear thinking and a general feeling of well-being.

At *any* time of the day you can realize: The rest of my life begins this moment!

When you are not in a state that you would wish to be in, you can mentally go to a more neutral place for a few moments and then choose a way of thinking, speaking, and acting that is consistent with your higher self.

If it is difficult to get to the neutral state, then focus on your breathing for the next few breaths. With each breath mentally or verbally express gratitude to our Creator for the oxygen that He is giving you right now to keep you alive.

Then ask yourself, "How do I want to be now?"

Try again to access the state of your choice, or pretend that you could. And then ask yourself, "If I could choose any way of speaking and acting now, what would I choose?"

The more practice you have with asking yourself this question and answering it, the easier it will become.

Congratulations. This very moment you begin the rest of your life. How do you want to be now?

> *I was speaking to someone who felt that he was not at his best for a long time. He was ready to tell me in detail about how he was not the way he wanted to be.*
>
> *"Wait a minute. You just told me the short version of what you don't want. We only have a limited amount of time to speak now. You can choose to use this time to inform me in detail, but right now, I feel that you will benefit much more*

if you describe what you do want to be."

"That makes sense to me," he said. As soon as he described his goals, the look on his face changed. His breathing was better. His facial expression was better. His posture was better.

"How do you feel right this moment?" I asked him.

"Much better than I have in a long time," he replied.

"Please note how easy that was for you. As your mind focuses on how you do want to behave, your entire mind-body goes into a much better state."

"But I don't think I can keep it up," he said. "What if later I go back to feeling bad again?"

"You will always be in a mind-body state that is consistent with that moment's thoughts. Of course, your past habits will come up again. But all you have to do is what you just did now: Think about how you want to be right now.

"You do want joy, courage, love for Hashem and other people and serenity, right?"

"Very much."

"So whenever you are not in a mind-body state that you would want for yourself, stop a moment and take a deep, grateful breath. Then think about how you do want to be and choose that way of being right now in the present.

"When you worry about how you will be later on, you are in your worried state, and that is not what you want for yourself. Say to yourself, 'Right now I can choose what to think, say, and do right now. Right now I can choose any thoughts, words, or actions that I would like to choose right now.'"

"But is it really so easy?" he asked.

"I don't blame you for not believing it. But I just saw you go into a positive state by thinking about how you do want to be. So I believe 100 percent that you can do it again.

"Be patient and be persistent. Every time you get yourself in a positive mind-body state by thinking about how you want to live, you will make it easier to believe that you can do it again. This is a skill like any other skill. The more you practice, the better you get.

"The slogan that will help you is, 'Right this moment, I am starting the rest of my life. And in order to get off to a great start I will think of the themes of Joy, Courage, Love, and Serenity.

"Don't argue with yourself why you can't always be this way. You don't have to try to always be this way. You just need to reflect for just one moment on the four words. Your mind-body will do the rest."

His expression showed that he would be putting himself in a positive state conducive for clear thinking.

Now, what does the Almighty want from me?

Your soul is on a mission from its Creator. You are unique. Only you are you, now and always. Only you have your unique life mission. Your loving Father and awesomely powerful Creator loves you and wants you to succeed.

The situations and occurrences throughout your life are Divinely orchestrated to elevate you and your character. The questions you ask yourself about life create you and get you to focus on a direction.

The Torah verse states (*Deuteronomy* 10:12): "And *now*, O Israel, what does the Almighty ask from you?" Please note the important word, "Now."

This is a question that we need to be aware of many times throughout each day. "Right now, what am I being asked to think, say, and do?"

Now, What Does the Almighty Want from Me? / 31

People who keep asking themselves, *What does the Almighty ask from me right now?*, will be on a path of elevating themselves spiritually.

This one question will make a major difference in all aspects of your life. It will enable you to free yourself from being upset about the past. Regardless of what you have or have not done in the past, the question to focus on is what you can do *now*.

This question will also free you from obsessing about what might be in the future. You might have a multitude of concerns about the future. You might have a multitude of plans. But the highest priority question for now is, "What can I do now that will be fulfilling the Almighty's will?"

Sometimes it will be very clear to you what the Almighty wants you to do. Other times, you will need to reflect and contemplate before you answer. At times, you might need to consult others. But at all times, you will be creating yourself in an elevated way.

Keep in mind that an important aspect of what the Almighty wants is for you to do His will with joy. Joy together with courage, love ("I love You, Hashem *Yisbarach*"), and serenity will help you stay on track.

> *Someone felt that he was far from the spiritual levels that he wanted to reach. He asked a student of the Chofetz Chaim for one piece of advice that would make a major difference in his life.*
>
> *The rabbi answered, "My teacher, the Chofetz Chaim, was known to be an elevated, righteous person. He was universally known to be a great tzaddik. What key factor made him into who he was? He always applied all that he learned. As soon as he learned something, from the time he was a young boy, he would ask himself, 'What does the Almighty want me to do now with what I have just learned?'*
>
> *"By emulating this one pattern," the rabbi concluded, "you will consistently develop yourself spiritually."*

Today is the greatest day of your life

Today is the greatest day of your life, because today is the only day that exists. All your earlier days are part of your mind's memory bank. All the future days haven't occurred yet. So today just has to be the greatest day of your life.

The way you experience the day will be different if you decide to view it as the greatest day of your life, right now. Today is the only day that you get to choose what you will think, say, and do today.

So think about it: What are some of the greatest thoughts that you could think on this great day in your life? What are some of the greatest things that you could say on this great day in your life? What are some of the greatest actions that you could do on this great day in your life?

Consider some great actions that you could possibly do. Even if you don't actually do them today, thinking about doing them elevates you today.

We never get to choose the exact nature of each day. The Almighty will send us unique challenges every single day. So the exact challenges that you experience today will be experienced only one time. Today is the only day of your life that you will be able to excel in utilizing today.

Since you are reading these words today, today you will be thinking about how to view today as the greatest day of your life. As you read this, you can't help reflecting on what it would mean if you considered this day as the greatest day of your life.

You have a choice. You might be able to say to yourself, *Today seems to be quite an ordinary day. I don't see how I can view today as the greatest day of my life*. If you think this way, you prevent yourself from viewing today as the greatest day of your life.

Or you might tell yourself, *Since I happen to be reading this today, perhaps there is a way that I can actually view today as the greatest day of my life*.

> People who strive for spiritual awareness will be able to keep growing and developing each day. This growth and development keeps adding up. When you take positive actions today, you now have more positive actions on your life's record books. Tomorrow, you will be able to do more good, but that will be how you view tomorrow. Today you only need to concern yourself how you view today.

When you gain more wisdom today, you will have more wisdom stored in your brain then ever before.

When you do an act of kindness today, you will have more acts of kindness stored in your personal life history than ever before.

May you have a great day today after contemplating how you can increase the greatness of today.

> "Today is going rough for me," the fellow said to me. "I can't view today as a great day."
>
> "Have you ever felt bad and then felt better?" I asked him.
>
> "Of course I have," he replied.
>
> "That means that in your life history, you know that you can feel bad and then feel good, isn't that correct?" I clarified.

"Certainly! But so what?"

"If you never have to feel bad that you feel bad, because you know that you will be able to feel better, that would be helpful, wouldn't it?"

"Yes, it would," he concurred.

"A while ago you felt bad. I see that you are feeling better now. You are now becoming a greater expert in going from feeling bad to feeling good. Continuing to gain greater expertise in being able to do this would keep making your life better, wouldn't it?"

"Definitely."

"Now just imagine how you would look at today. Imagine that you knew that today you realized that your thoughts are up to you, and that you can change your mood from feeling bad to feeling good whenever you need this skill. That would make today a great day, wouldn't it?"

"But it's still not the greatest day of my life," he protested.

"But it is a great day. And viewing today as a great day is a step up from viewing it as a tough day, isn't it?"

"That's amazing. I see how I can transform today into a great day. And if I adapt this pattern, each day will be a great day."

The book of your life is made up of a multitude of short stories

We each have a story of our life. How we choose to label the story will have a major impact on whether we will experience much happiness or much sadness.

Two people might have very similar life experiences, but one person will keep his main focus on the things that he was happy about, while the other focuses on the opposite. One person focuses mainly on his achievements and successes, and how he can keep developing himself and achieving even more in the future. The other person focuses mainly on his failures and limitations. One person's life is full of gratitude and appreciation, while the other person's life is full of resentment and regrets.

How you label the main theme of your life is the key to whether you live a life of spiritual growth and fulfillment, or a life of materialism and disappointment.

The very fact that you are alive means that your life is still a story in process. Regardless of your "early chapters," you can upgrade the nature of your life's story from now on. Regardless of how you initially react in any situation or circumstance, you can wisely choose to grow from every challenge.

Right at this moment you can say to yourself, *From now on, I will keep my main focus on the good that I can do. I will constantly refine my character traits, and I will keep making elevating choices.*

Each day you make a multitude of choices. Your life is made up of one short story after another.

Keep asking yourself questions like these:

What is the wisest thing to say and do next?

How can I grow spiritually with my choices of thoughts, words, and actions right now?

If I were to make a determined effort to become an elevated person, what would I think, say, and do now?

What would my Father, my King, Creator and Sustainer of the universe, want me to say and do now?

When I'll look back at my life, what would I have wished that I had said or done? Right now I will develop a plan to say and do those things.

In any given situation, no matter how challenging it is, you only have to deal with today. And today you only have to deal with now.

You might feel that it's hard to keep up a positive and wise way of being. But you don't have to be positive and wise all day: you only need to be positive and wise right now, one moment at a time.

Look at your life as the story of a great person. Every day, choose a number of moments that are an expression of a great way of being. These great moments add up. They create a great life.

> *A fellow told me that he was disappointed with the way his life was unfolding. As he was getting older, he felt worse and worse. He knew that he was basically a good person, but he felt that his life was passing by. He wasn't outstanding in any way. He didn't have any major life achievements. He wasn't focused on impressing anyone else, but he wanted to feel more satisfied and fulfilled himself.*

"When you think of your life as a story, what would you consider the theme?" I asked him.

"The life of a mediocre fellow," he said.

"I am going to give you an assignment. View each new day as another page in your autobiography. You can call your life story, 'A meaningful life.' Each day ask yourself, 'What are three things I can do today that I would consider meaningful?'"

When I spoke to him about a week later, he reported, "So far this has been extremely helpful for me. I actually do many more than three meaningful things a day. I now realize that I have always done many meaningful things, but that wasn't the way that I summarized my life. Now that I am viewing my life as the story of a meaningful life, I see that I do plenty of meaningful things each day.

"My goal is to keep up this awareness. I have begun a journal of meaningful things that I have done. I am more aware of my connection with the Almighty. I am more aware of the kindnesses that I do. I am more aware of my developing positive traits. I realize that I don't need to write an autobiography that will be interesting for anyone else to read. I want to live my life in a meaningful way. When I keep my mind on this concept, I feel so much better about my whole life."

Over time, he continued reporting his gratitude for the major impact that this focus had on his entire way of being.

Accept what you feel now and you will be open to better feelings in a moment

Many times we don't feel as positive as we might wish. In those moments, the wisest thing is to accept whatever we are feeling.

When you accept your current feeling, you will be more open to feeling better in a moment from now.

Remember this general rule: Whenever you aren't satisfied with how you feel, you are thinking of current dissatisfaction. A moment ago you read that last sentence and you are in a new present moment. In the present, the feelings you didn't like a moment ago are now in the past. You can't change the past. But you can choose wisely in the present, right now. So ask yourself: *What would I like to think and feel right now?*

It isn't helpful to try to fight and resist feelings that aren't joyful. A friend of mine told me that 40 years ago, Rabbi Nosson Wachtfogel, the *mashgiach* of Lakewood, told him this principle when he was upset over something and had unsuccessfully tried to fight those feelings. Once my friend heard that he didn't have to resist what he was feeling, he felt much more at ease. He immediately felt better.

Of course you want to feel joyful. That's the way our Creator created us. When you are joyful, your brainwaves and immune system work at optimal levels. Your neurotransmitters enable you to think with greater clarity. You are brighter and smarter when you are in a joyful state.

When we are not joyful, we would choose joy if we could. But sometimes we feel emotionally stuck. We try to feel better but it doesn't always work. So logically we keep trying to feel better.

But this isn't the way most brains and minds work. By calmly accepting what we feel in the present, even if we wish it were different, our minds can make better choices in a few moments from now.

If you are skilled at changing your feelings with your thoughts, keep using your skill. If not, it's not a problem. You don't need to *change*. You just need to *choose* better and wiser now. For many people the thought of *choosing better and wiser now* makes the process much easier.

You can't really change what you felt in the past, even the past of a moment ago. But you can choose better now. When you choose better thoughts, words, and action right now, you will feel better.

> *After my class about increasing the joy in your life, someone told me, "I do feel joyful once in a while. But I frequently feel very unhappy. I have valid reasons for feeling the way I do. What can I do about it?"*
>
> *I told him that I would tell him something that would be helpful to him, even if others are not able to apply it.*
>
> *I said, "Embrace your down feelings with joy. There are many spiritual reasons why your down feelings will serve you. But when you are feeling emotionally stuck in distress,*

your mind will not be working as well as when you are calmly objective. So to make it easier for you, just imagine that you could do this with a sense of humor at the irony of the whole situation.

"Say to your down feelings. 'I welcome you, my down feelings, with joy. I hope you don't stay long. I wish for you to go away. But right now I greet you with a hearty welcome. Enjoy your short stay.'

"Then allow yourself to feel totally whatever you are feeling. As long as you don't add any negative thoughts about those feelings, you will be surprised at how they become lighter and eventually go away.

"If they still stay, start laughing. You might say to them, 'This is funny. I don't know why but this reminds me of times I've laughed and couldn't stop laughing.'"

The fellow thought this was a funny thing to do and started laughing. "That laughter makes you feel a little better, doesn't it?" I asked.

"Now that I notice it, I can see that I do feel better. I'll remember this."

What would be the best state for now?

We all think, speak, and act better when we are in our best mind-body states. We all think, speak, and act worse when we are in our worst mind-body states.

For instance, reflect on how you interact with someone when you feel vitally alive, energized, cheerful, and friendly. Now reflect on how you interact with that same person when you feel frustrated, tired, hungry, and in a totally miserable mood.

You speak and act differently, don't you?

Reflect on a time that you were performing in any capacity in front of other people when you felt vibrantly alive, energized, self-confident, and flowing. Compare that to your performance when you felt exhausted, worn out, insecure, and distracted. If you can't recall a specific instance, just imagine performing in the positive mind-body state and then imagine performing in the negative mind-body state.

You speak and act differently, don't you?

Reflect on praying when you feel inspired, elevated, and connected to your Father, your King, Creator and Sustainer of the universe. Then reflect on trying to pray when you are worn out and distracted.

You pray differently, don't you?

Reflect on studying when your mind is clear and you are easily able to concentrate and focus on what you are studying. Now compare that with trying to study when you are in a stuck mind-body state.

You study differently, don't you?

When you are about to do something, take a moment to allow yourself to enter the best mind-body state for that activity.

When you are about to perform in any capacity, ask yourself, *What would be the best state for me to be in when I perform now?*

If you are not in the state that you wish to be in, don't think thoughts that will make you feel even worse. Rather, choose the thoughts and actions that are conducive to being in your best state. Just choose the best appropriate state that you are capable of accessing right now. You will be in a better state than if you engaged in counterproductive self-talk.

The more you practice creating high-performance states, the easier it will be for you to flow into these states more often.

[Please note: There are many brain and body changes when we are in various states. I speak about states frequently and have listed these alphabetically: B.B.B.E.H.H.I.M.P.T. This refers to Blood pressure, Brainwaves, Breathing style, Energy level, Heartbeats, Hormones (the biochemistry changes when we are in a positive state such as joy or bliss, or a distressful state such as fear or stress), Immune system (which functions better when we are in joyful or serene states), Muscle tension, Physiology (posture and facial expression), Tone of voice.

So a change in state is not a minor distinction. Rather, many of our systems are affected. Giving unique positive names to your positive states will remind you of times that you have already been in these states. Unique names make it easier to access various states that are already stored in your brain.

Changing physiology, that is, your body posture and facial expression, is a quick way to change your state. In 1740, many years before the extent of our brainwave and biochemistry change was known, Rabbi Moshe Chaim Luzzatto wrote in the classic *mussar* work *Mesilas Yesharim* (Ch. 7): "External movements stimulate inner changes." He was referring to speaking and acting with great enthusiasm for prayer and other spiritual practices.]

> "I am a person who has many different moods," someone said to me. "When I am in a good mood everything seems to go so much better for me. Professionally and personally, when I am in a good mood my mind thinks clearly and creatively. I feel a strong sense of well-being and I accomplish what I set out to accomplish.
>
> "Unfortunately, when I am in a bad mood, nothing seems to go right. My self-image is contemptible. I feel bad about myself. I worry about the future. I make many mistakes and errors. It's almost like I am a totally different person."
>
> "The majority of people think, speak, and act so much better when they are in a positive state," I replied. "The first step toward improving is to realize what state you are in when you want to speak to someone or perform in any way.
>
> "One of the most important states to master is the state that I refer to as centered, focused, and flowing. When you are centered, your mind and body are in a calm, clear-thinking state. When you are focused, you think for a moment about what you need to say or do. When you are flowing, you naturally are in the best state for that moment. You have greater access to the magnificent library in your brain. Every good moment in your life is stored there, together will all your knowledge accumulated over your entire life.
>
> "Some people refer to this state as a high-performance state. Others refer to it as being in the zone. You can call this state whatever you would like to call it. The name of the state isn't important. It's how you think, feel, speak, and act in this state that counts.

"Based on what you told me about yourself, I think that for you it might be best to call it, 'At my ultimate best' state."

"Just hearing this put me into a great state," he said.

"Then you might call it, 'My greatest state.'" I suggested. This worked wonders for him.

Act now the way you wish to be

We all have patterns of speaking and acting. We also have an ideal self: the way we wish to be. Unnecessarily limiting thoughts hold people back from becoming their ideal self. They basically think: *I would really like to be "this" way. But the reality is that I am not like "this."*

The truth is, if you have an ideal "way of being," in mind, you can speak and act in ways consistent with that ideal right now. Since right now you are in this present moment, and in this present moment you can choose to speak and act any way you choose, you always have the magnificent ability to speak and act the way you wish to be.

Using the three time periods, there are three focuses that convince us not to speak and act in our ideal manner.

One way is to focus on the past. "I have not regularly spoken and acted in this way in the past. Therefore I choose not to speak and act that way right now."

Another way is to focus on the future. "I would really like to speak and act in this ideal way. But right now it seems impossible, or at least very difficult, for me to consistently speak and act in this ideal way. Therefore I choose not to start speaking and acting that way right now."

And the third way is to focus on the present but to think, *I would really like to speak and act in this ideal way, but it's just not the way I really am. Therefore I refuse to speak and act in this ideal way right now.*

Stop stopping yourself. Speak and act in ways consistent with your ideal self right now.

It is important to realize, "My identity is only an imaginary concept of how I choose to view myself right now. My choice in the present can override any limiting mental thought."

Choose to speak and act with joy right now.

Choose to speak and act with courage right now.

Choose to speak and act with love for Hashem and love for kindness right now.

Choose to speak and act with serenity right now.

Keep asking yourself, *How would I ideally like to act, if I could choose any ideal way right now?* Then actually speak and act that way.

> *A former student of mine told me, "I had a very limiting way of being. I had a very negative self-image. I looked at myself as neurotic. I had obsessive tendencies, a short attention span, and I was highly impulsive.*
>
> *"I am very grateful to you for telling me that I had the ability to speak and act any way that I chose. Even if I didn't think I could keep it up, right now I could speak and act that way, like an actor on stage. I could pretend that I could speak and act like the wonderful person that I secretly wished I were.*
>
> *"You told me that the longer I spoke and acted in ideal ways in the present, the more chance there was that I could maintain it. But, you said, if I never start, I will never be that way. Starting doesn't guarantee that I will be consistent. But*

it does mean that I have a real possibility of speaking and acting in better ways.

"I love imitating people. You told me that this ability, which every young child has, is the ability that can enable me to create myself any way that I wished. I should stop stopping myself and start speaking and acting that way.

"By looking at the positive way of being as only make-believe, I stopped blocking myself. Today I am a much-improved human being. You told me I didn't really need to believe that I could be this way, I just had to speak and act this way in the present. You told me to have fun and enjoy the process. I decided to take you up on it. This changed my life. Words can't express how grateful I feel."

What can I do now to move forward on my priority goals?

Making and reaching high-priority goals creates a meaningful life. This is one of the most important concepts for anyone who truly wants to live a happy life. Certainly, gratitude is an important element in happiness. Kindness is another important element. But together with gratitude and kindness, a life devoted to high-priority goals is a vital element for happiness.

At different stages in their lives, people will have diverse goals to focus on. As our life situation changes, the nature of our high-priority goals will change also.

Our essence is our soul. Therefore our spiritual goals should be high on our goal list. Regardless of our specific situation and the conditions of our life, we always need to devote thoughts and actions to strive for our highest priority spiritual goals.

Everyone has spiritual goals they strive to reach. Healthy people and people who aren't healthy have spiritual goals. So do people who are wealthy and people who aren't. So do people who are young and people who are elderly. So do people who are single and people who are married. So do people who find life going relatively smoothly and people who are faced with daily challenges.

Developing our character and the emotional quality of our life are spiritual goals. Along with any other goals we set for ourselves, we should remember to daily strive for *tikun hamidos*, refinement of our character.

At any given moment of our lives we would be wise to ask, "What can I do now to move forward on my priority goals?"

> *In a class I gave on setting goals, someone asked me, "What do you consider the chief challenge people face when they focus on their goals?"*
>
> *I replied, "There is a common challenge for people who sincerely work toward the goals they set for themselves. That is, it's easy for them to think that they'll only be able to be happy and have peace of mind when they reach their goals. But until then, they expect to feel a sense of incompleteness.*
>
> *"Allowing himself to feel good only when he reaches a goal will doom him to constant frustration because he always has a new goal in mind. He doesn't allow himself to enjoy his progress.*
>
> *"The solution: Be totally resolved to be joyful and serene on your journey to reach a goal. Each moment of life is precious. Each moment of life is a gift. Remember to come back to the joy of being alive. Remember this before you reach any other goal you set for yourself. And remember this after you reach any goal. Once a goal is reached, after the initial joy, you will only feel good if you focus on gratitude. Don't wait until you successfully reach a goal. Allow yourself to experience joy during the entire process of going for any goal."*

Later on, someone who had attended the class said, "You were talking to the other fellow, but I immediately realized that this is exactly what I needed to hear. I am extremely grateful. I feel better now than I have ever felt in my life."

To concentrate, focus your total attention on what you are doing now

Totally focusing on the present moment is the key to concentration. Thoughts about the past, be they positive or negative, prevent concentration. Similarly, worrying about the future keeps your mind away from the present moment. Thinking about anything but the immediate task at hand is distracting.

Integrating the message that "life is now" will make it easier to keep your mind focused on the present. This attitude will help you concentrate on what is right before you.

To study effectively, we need to focus our total attention on what we are reading. To listen wholeheartedly, we need to focus our total attention on what someone is saying. To pray with all our heart and all our soul, we need to focus our total attention on the words we are saying to the Almighty.

Getting upset at yourself for a lack of concentration is not conducive to focusing. If your mind wanders when you need to focus, calmly bring your mind back to the present. This is a skill that you can build up with practice.

Repeat the word "Focus," to train your mind. Place your finger on the line you're reading when you repeat the word, "Focus." Remaining calm and serene also makes it easier to stay focused.

Give yourself positive feedback for each success. You are likely to find that it will speed up the process when you explicitly say, "Great!" after bringing back your wandering attention.

There are two major areas of focus: exterior and interior. Focusing on what is happening outside of you means you are concentrating on what you are hearing and seeing now. Focusing on what is going on inside of you means you are paying attention to your thoughts and feelings.

You can switch back and forth by giving your mind instructions. Say, "Outside," when you want to focus on what you are seeing and hearing. Say, "Inside," when you want to focus on your own thoughts and feelings.

"I joyfully focus right now," is an affirmation that will increase both your level of focus and your positive feelings.

> *Someone who used to find it very difficult to concentrate well when trying to study and read shared an approach that worked well for him.*
>
> *"When I was in school, I was an awful student. I hated to study and I avoided doing homework whenever I could. My attention span tended to be short when I wasn't interested in a subject, which included the vast majority of what my teachers attempted to teach me in school. But when I was engaged in doing something that I was truly interested in, I could concentrate for long periods of time.*
>
> *"But once I was finished with formal schooling, I realized that I would need to concentrate for longer periods of time to get and keep a job. The solution I found was that I could concentrate well for short bursts of time. Ten minutes at a time was about it. After every ten minutes, I would mentally*

take a break for at least a minute, and then I was ready to concentrate and focus for another ten minutes. When possible, I chose to focus on some other aspect of what I needed to concentrate on. Concentrating for ten minute segments at a time worked so well for me that I got a lot more accomplished than many others who could concentrate for longer periods of time in one shot."

See and hear what you can see and hear right now

Our thoughts easily wander to things that were said and done in the past and to things that might be said or done in the future. Sometimes we might find it difficult to focus properly on the task at hand. Other times we cause ourselves a lot of needless distress by thinking painful thoughts about the past or future. Here is a tool to help us come back to the present: Actively notice what is going on around us.

When you objectively observe what you are seeing or hearing, your mind is focused on the present moment. One of the simplest ways to get your mind to focus on this present moment is to say to yourself, *Right now I am aware of seeing...(something near you)* or *Right now I am aware of hearing...(a specific sound)* You can even say to yourself, *Right now as I scan myself from head to toe, I am aware of feeling muscle tension in my ... (neck, jaws, forehead, or any other set of muscles)*.

If necessary, you can say five to ten sentences that begin with the words, "Right now I am aware of …" This will bring your conscious awareness to the present moment. Then you can choose to think about any beneficial thought.

> *"I am a high-school teacher and one of my main challenges is how to get my students to concentrate on the lesson that I am teaching. When I was a student, my biggest challenge was boredom. When I am fascinated with a topic or subject, I can concentrate for a long time. But when I am bored, I have trouble concentrating. I first started teaching a number of years ago, and I feel that those students were able to concentrate better than my current students. I am always looking for what I can do to help my students concentrate better.*
>
> *"The best advice I heard was that I should show greater enthusiasm for my subject. When I am enthusiastic, it comes through in my voice and my mannerisms.*
>
> *"The next best piece of advice was the suggestion that from time to time, I should suggest to my class, 'Right now, let's all take a two-minute break. Let's breathe deeply. Let's exhale all stress and tension. And let's breathe in healthy oxygen for our brains and all the trillions of cells in our bodies. Now, let's all become more aware of what we are seeing and hearing right now in this moment. Now, let's all say together, "Right now, I am aware of the teacher talking." "Right now, I am aware of what is to my right." "Right now, I am aware of what is to my left." "Right now, I am aware of what is in front of me when I look up." "Right now, I am aware of the text on my desk."'*
>
> *"I have found that this is very helpful for getting my students to mentally return to the here and now and pay attention to what I am teaching."*

Curiosity each day: "what will be today's highlights?"

The start of each day is a great time to condition your mind to be on the lookout for the most joyful, inspiring, and spiritual experiences of the day. At the start of each day we are given a body and a soul as a gift from our Creator. We can make many great choices and decisions.

Every single day of your life has its highlights. When we wake up in the morning and reflect on the joy of being alive, we can wonder with curiosity, "What will be the greatest highlights of my day today?"

Each day has its unique opportunities for connecting with our Father, our King, Creator and Sustainer of the universe. We can connect through regular prayer and personal prayers, through gratitude and appreciation, and through joy and love.

Each day has its unique opportunities for character development and refinement.

Each day has its unique opportunities for kindness and compassion in words and deeds.

Each day has its unique opportunities for reviewing ideas and learning new concepts.

Each day is a brand-new day of challenges and tests. Each challenge and test can be dealt with and handled with the most positive and wisest resources we already have stored in our amazing brains. We can also create new patterns and innovative solutions. We can consult others for suggestions and ideas. We can research through books and articles.

At the start of each day we can never know exactly how the day will unfold. But we can mentally prepare ourselves in advance to think at our best and wisest.

Be prepared to recognize the best moments of each day. Consciously say to yourself, *I am going to add this moment to the highlights of my day list.* At the end of the day, review the highlights of that day.

When you seek them, you will notice many best moments. You might even actively create them.

> "My life is far from the way I wish it were," the student said to me. "I am already 22 years old, and some of my friends are already married. I feel far from ready to get married. A number of people have told me to work on my self-esteem and also on my emotions. I'm afraid that the entire process will take way too long. What can I do?"
>
> "There is a major difference between just focusing on what's wrong, and focusing on what needs to be done to improve and correct a situation," I told him.
>
> "To feel better and upgrade your self-image, get yourself a notebook. Each day write down at least five highlights for that day. This can be moments of joy, moments of insight, moments when you spoke or acted with greater courage than usual, moments of self-discipline and self-control, moments of joyful willpower. You can list breakthroughs in any area that is important to you," I suggested.
>
> The fellow reported that as the highlights kept adding up,

his self-confidence and total self-image kept growing. He looked forward to adding to his Highlight Journal.
   I would highly suggest that you do the same.

Regardless of your past self-image, right now you can see yourself in a better light

Your sense of identity plays a major role in your life. We tend to speak and act in ways that are consistent with our view of who we are.

As you read this now, you have a self-image about how old you are. People usually don't mention days when discussing their age, yet every day adds to your self-image of your age. Young children, however, do tend to say "and a half." Just as you add days to your self-image about your age, you can add other concepts to your self-image each and every day.

You have a self-image about what goals are reasonable for you and what goals are not. As you continue to gain more knowledge and develop more skills, you improve your self-image of what you know and what you can do.

Some individuals believe they are more skilled than they really are. But in our generation, there are more people who don't believe in themselves as much as they should. Be realistic. Be open to the objective feedback from knowledgeable people. And keep upgrading your thoughts about what you can do.

You have a self-image about how happy you usually are. You have a self-image about how much courage or fear you have. You have a self-image about how calm and serene you are, or how nervous and full of anxiety. Every happy moment can add to your self-image of how much happiness you have stored in your brain. The same applies to your moments of courage and serenity, patience, persistence, determination, kindness, and so forth.

The most important issue is whether a person has a positive self-image about his value and worth. Some people feel that they lack self-esteem. Some feel that they lack real worth and value.

Regardless of what you have considered your self-image yesterday or even this morning, you do not have to continue to view yourself the same way. Right now, at this moment, you can upgrade the way you view yourself.

Right now, you have the freewill choice of realizing that you are immensely valuable. You are created in the image of the Creator and Sustainer of the universe. You are a child of the Creator. You are a precious soul who has been put in this world to fulfill a unique mission.

Right now you can gain a greater realization that if you have thought, spoken, or acted in a way that is consistent with a positive pattern, those memories are always with you. Every good deed you do today is added to the eternal storehouse of all the good that you have done.

Building your self-image is a lifelong process. Each and every day you are adding to who you are. Of course we all have our moments of being up and moments of being down. But we always have intrinsic worth and value. Our emotions fluctuate, but our value is constant.

Mistakes and errors need to be learned from and corrected. To keep improving, we need to learn from the feedback of all the important things that we try to do. Focus on the joy and pleasure of making progress.

Remember this beneficial self-talk about your self-image: "I will view each day as a gift from my Creator. Right now, I am grateful to my Creator for all the good that I have experienced from the day I was born until this moment. Each and every day I gain more knowledge and wisdom. Each and every day I am committed to adding to the good that I can do. As long as I am alive, I will keep growing and developing my character. I will see myself as a soul who is on a Divine mission. My goal is to love my Creator and to love other people. I wish to bring joy to my Creator and joy to other people."

> Someone called me up and said, "I have been told that I have low self-esteem and as long as I keep up this negative attitude, I will be a failure for the rest of my life. I feel awful. What can I do?"
>
> I suggested that he read my book Building Your Self-Image and the Self-Image of Others to find helpful ideas.
>
> I advised, "The main thing is to realize that you are on a process of building your self-image. Please repeat after me: 'My goal is to build my self-image each and every day. I will stop saying that I have low self-esteem. Right now is now and not before now. And now I am resolved to keep building who I am.'"
>
> "I'm not sure that I will be able to keep building myself," he said hesitantly.
>
> "You told me you feel awful when you think about not having self-esteem. And you made this phone call, right?"
>
> "Yes. But what does that prove?"
>
> "It proves that you are willing to try to do something to feel better. I would like a one-week commitment from you. Commit that you will stop saying that you have low self-esteem. For this entire week, say to yourself, 'Right now I am in the process of building my self-image. My self-image grows with each positive thing that I do.'"

I asked, "Can you feel now that it makes sense to experiment and see if this self-talk about your self-image is helpful?"

The fellow started reading the book and kept his one-week commitment. He said in a later conversation, "That's the end of my repeating that I have low self-esteem. I am now going to move forward with creating myself with my new picture of who I am."

Every encounter with another person happens in the here and now

Before you speak to someone, you have that ability to say to yourself, *Right now, what is the wisest and best way for me to interact with this person?*

Certainly we all have patterns of how we speak and act in general and how we speak and act with specific individuals. Perhaps a certain person is challenging and difficult to speak with. You might have found yourself frustrated or irritated or actually angry when talking to him. But now in the present, you can choose to be wiser than ever before and upgrade your interaction with him. You can select any pattern. You can be kinder right now. You can be more understanding right now. You can be more compassionate right now. You can be at your most elevated right now.

Every time you interact with another person you are interacting in the present moment. This means that during any "now" interaction with anyone, you are more knowledgeable and experienced than ever before.

For example, after you read this entire book you will have more moments of joy, courage, love, and serenity stored in your brain. This can help you make better and wiser choices of what to say and do. Perhaps you weren't at your best and wisest when you spoke to someone before. But now you might be able to speak and act better than last time.

People might expect you to speak and act in ways consistent with their previous encounters with you. But if you realize you will gain from speaking and acting in better ways than ever before, you have the freewill ability to choose to speak and act in better ways. In addition, when you speak and act at your wisest and best, the other person is more likely to speak and act in ways that are better than ever before.

If you already speak and act in positive ways, right now you can still choose to speak and act in even better ways.

Right now, think of someone you would like to interact with better than before. What would you like to say to this person if you could upgrade your communication pattern? Mentally practice saying it. Perhaps you could write it down and then edit what you will say. Maybe you can record what you want to say and then listen to what you recorded. Ask yourself, *How can I say this even better?* Continue to practice saying it until you are satisfied with the improvement.

You can't control anyone else's way of speaking and acting. But by upgrading your own way of speaking and acting, you are more likely to bring out a better way of being in the other person.

Even if you have positive interactions with certain people, you might be able to have an even better interaction now. Think of a specific example of how you can apply this pattern.

> *A student of mine told me that he was having problems with a few students from a different school who lived in his neighborhood. They seemed to enjoy making fun of him.*

That got him angry and he insulted them back. Of course, that just made things worse and they had an ongoing verbal feud.

"I not only feel bad about the way they treat me," he said. "I also feel bad about the way that I speak to them. I keep stooping to their level and I feel guilty for doing so. This pattern has been going on for a while already. I'm afraid that it has already become a deep-seated habit. What can I do about it?"

I replied, "The very fact that you feel bad about speaking badly to them is a positive message about your values. It's easy to blame someone else for the way that we interact with them. 'They started it. If they would speak better to me, I would speak better to them.'

"Realizing that you have a freewill choice now in the present can help you upgrade the way you interact with them. When you think about them in the present, if you were at your wisest and best, how would you want to interact?"

"I would like to treat them with respect and I would want them to treat me with respect," he replied.

"Great! In Avos D'Reb Noson it states that a mighty person is one who transforms an enemy into a friend. It takes a major act of spiritual courage to refrain from bearing a grudge and saying things that maintain the hostility. It takes even more spiritual courage to actually be kind and treat someone as an authentic friend. It takes inner effort. But the fruit of your investment is that you can change an erstwhile foe into a loyal friend.

"I know that you are sincere in your desire to act in a more elevated way. The only way one can become skilled at a difficult skill is to practice and keep on practicing.

"Picture yourself speaking and acting toward those fellows the way you would toward a good friend. In the beginning they might be skeptical. But as you keep it up, your words and actions will convey the message that you are extending your hand in friendship. They will eventually improve the way they interact with you.

"The history of the way you have interacted in the past doesn't have to prevent you from acting at your best and bringing out the best in them. Put in the effort and give me feedback on how it worked out."

A few days later he reported to me. "I wouldn't have believed it if I hadn't seen it myself. They now treat me better than I could ever have imagined."

Everything is perfect right now

Right now, in each present moment, your life is perfect for you to continue fulfilling your life's mission. Each moment of life provides you with opportunities to develop your character and elevate your life.

Some moments will give you exactly the experience you would want. Grow from each of these moments. Some experiences will not be exactly what you would choose. You may wish to be someplace else or to do something different at that moment. Grow from each of these moments. Some moments will seem O.K., but you may wish for something more enjoyable or meaningful. Grow from each of these moments as well.

Your thoughts can make every moment meaningful. Every moment, you can fulfill the commandment of expressing love for the Creator ("I love You, Hashem *Yisbarach*").

The more challenging the situations and circumstances are, the greater the opportunity to develop your character.

In every present moment, ask, "What is the perfect, wisest and most meaningful thing I can think, say, or do right now?"

A student said to me, "My theme for living seems to be, 'I wish I were living a different life.' I keep thinking about how I wish things were in my life. This creates many moments of frustration."

I replied, "I have a suggestion. Experience the rest of the day as being perfect for what you need to fulfill your purpose for living. You can't magically be someone else and be somewhere else. But within the context of your present reality, think thoughts of elevating your life. Change what can be changed. Think higher thoughts while you do whatever needs to be done today."

The next day he said to me, "It's amazing how nothing changed and everything changed. I did things that I have done many times. But yesterday everything was transformed. I wish I could keep it up."

I suggested, "Each day repeat to yourself a number of times, 'Today is perfect for my mission in life.' This will give you many more similar 'perfect' experiences."

Having enough for today gives you an abundant life today

Having enough money is a high priority for people who must support themselves, their families, and others. Part of the challenge is that even when we have enough for right now, we still need to think about what will be later.

It's possible for a person to live 80 or 90 years and still worry each day about having enough money. Every single day of his life, he could have had a place to live, have had enough food, and have met all of his basic needs. Nevertheless, he may experience much worry and anxiety about managing in the future.

Looking back at their lives, these elderly people could easily say, "Isn't it amazing how all that I've worried about was for nothing? If only I had known that I would always have enough for each and every day of my life, I wouldn't have had to worry."

The good news is that no one has to worry. Worry doesn't help you. Planning and thinking clearly about what you can do can be beneficial. But causing yourself the distress of worry is unnecessary suffering.

What does abundance mean? At the simplest level, abundance means that you have your needs met right now.

Most people could create a sense of abundance by consistently living life one day at a time. Then they can ask, "Are my basic needs met right now?" When your answer is, "Yes," then appreciate the abundance that you do have.

You only can live at one time: today. Rejoice and celebrate when you have what you need for today. This way you will be able to experience a sense of abundance each and every day.

Gain the benefits of living with abundance one day at a time. Some people are so worried about the future that they forget to experience the full benefits of abundance day by day.

Remember this rule: Having enough for today gives you abundance for today. Imagine how much you will benefit from living with this attitude.

> *An elderly gentleman once told me, "I am a pessimist. I have a tendency to think that the worst will happen. I worry a lot. And even when things do turn out much better than I had feared, I continue to worry that bad things will happen now.*
>
> *"Whenever I hear a prediction about a food shortage, I worry that the shortage will begin much sooner than expected. When there are fears of financial collapse, I assume that there is a good chance that I will lose my entire life savings."*
>
> *"Do your adult children think the same way you do?" I asked him.*
>
> *"I am grateful that they don't. They have told me that growing up in our house was scary. They frequently heard me say that there will be major shortages very soon. They heard me worry about how we will manage when things get really bad. But things never really got that bad. As my oldest son told me, 'I finally realized that this extreme pessimism caused much needless suffering. Even if things did get as*

bad as you worried they would, I can still enjoy what I have today.'

"I told my son that I am proud of him for having this attitude. But it's just not the way that I think."

I asked this man if he would like to become more appreciative for what he does have. "Of course, I would," he said. "Who wouldn't? But I have this bad habit for so many years, that I don't see myself changing."

"Even if you don't really expect to change, perhaps you could spend just a few days being grateful for the abundance that you do have?" I suggested.

"I think I could do that for a day or two," he agreed.

The fellow was an interesting character. He never really "changed." But he was willing to continue experimenting with feeling grateful for the abundance that the Almighty gave him for a few more days. These "few days" lasted much longer than the fellow expected.

Everything before now is your present past: elevate it in your mind

What was the future this morning is now part of your past. You can't redo the past. If you thought, felt, said, or did something before this moment, you already thought, felt, said, or did it.

Regardless of what you already thought, felt, said, or did before the next moment, you can still choose to think great thoughts now, feel great feelings now, say great things now, and do great things now.

You can also mentally elevate your past thoughts and actions. You can look back at the past and use your present level of love for the Creator and love for other people, and think about the choices you would now make in those past situations. Using your present knowledge and wisdom, you can imagine yourself speaking and acting at your best and your wisest in those past situations.

Reviewing the past situations and encounters with your present wisdom can enlighten your soul right now. You are also filling your subconscious mind with your present knowledge and awareness. This gives you added inner resources for the future.

Your past now includes even more thoughts, words, and actions. And there is no limit to how high a level you can elevate it. Your awareness of potential spiritual, emotional, and practical possibilities will keep growing. And with each new present realization, you will be able to develop both your past and your future even more.

> Someone I encountered complained, "I grew up being told very often, 'Every missed opportunity is lost for good.'
>
> " The people telling me this meant well. They wanted to motivate me to take advantage of every opportunity that came my way. But this phrase caused tremendous distress. I constantly regretted all the opportunities I had lost out on in the past.
>
> "I started to feel bad every time I learned a valuable concept and idea.
>
> "My thoughts would go, 'You could and should have known this before. Look at how much you already lost out by not applying this a long time ago.'
>
> "The more I learned, the worst I felt."
>
> I told the fellow that he could rectify this in one of two ways.
>
> One approach would be to be grateful: Now that he knew this concept, he could look forward to applying it from now on. Even if he only applied it once in a while, he would still gain a lot. He could be joyful while anticipating his gains and accomplishments with this idea in the future. This way he would feel good whenever he learned something to apply when opportunities arose.
>
> He could also gain by visualizing himself applying the new idea when appropriate in the past. This pretend application would upgrade his past memories. The more often he

imagined behaving that way in the past, the deeper impression this idea would make. This will enable him to act that way more easily in the present.

Even if you don't yet feel capable of inserting the new idea into your mental pictures of your past, you can apply it to the present and visualize it when you think about the future.

Right now I am alive, and I release all stress and tension

Right now you are alive and you are breathing. And right now you are reading about releasing stress and tension. Every time you read about releasing stress and tension, you are reminded that you have the ability to release stress and tension when you desire.

Releasing stress and tension has been compared to releasing an object from your hands. Every time you carry any object and put it down, your fingers curl and then uncurl to release the object. This is similar to the process that you go through when you release stress and tension from your muscles.

We don't know exactly how we tighten and loosen the muscles in our hands that enable us to pick things up and let them go. But we all know we can do it. We did this when we were infants, before we could speak, and we can still do it.

When you breathe slowly and deeply, your muscles automatically relax. So whenever you are aware that you are tense or are experiencing stress, remember to breathe deeply. Be grateful for each breath. As you continue breathing deeply, you will release even more stress and tension.

When you release stress and tension, your mind and body and all your systems are open to more moments of joy, courage, kindness, and serenity.

All stress and tension is created in your mind. The same way that imagining something dangerous immediately causes you to tense up, just imagining a calm and relaxing place can create calm, relaxed feelings.

Right now, imagine a very calm and peaceful place. This could be a place that you once visited. It could even be an imaginary place that you create right now in your mind.

Describe a calm and relaxing scene. It might be a beautiful garden. Since you are creating it in your mind, you can have as many flowers and trees as you want in your mental garden. If you like, you can add relaxing music. Either play relaxing music now or remember relaxing music that you once heard.

Hear a calming and relaxing voice saying to you, "Right now, you can let go of all stress and tension."

Tell yourself out loud, "Right now I am in the process of letting go of all stress and tension."

Right now, breathe as if you just put down a very heavy package you were carrying. This form of breathing releases tension.

You might be able to let go of all stress and tension right away or little by little. Each deep breath releases even more stress and tension. Even when you think of other things while breathing, your mind and body will subconsciously be in the process of releasing more stress and tension, enabling you to become calmer and calmer.

Mastering the skill of becoming calmer and thinking more clearly is one of the healthiest skills we can learn. People who mastered this skill have healed their health conditions created by stress.

Whenever you see an infant in a serene state, your mind can say, "I too was once an infant. I too had many moments of serenity when I was young. Right now, I let go of all unnecessary thoughts that are not calm and serene."

As you keep building up a greater appreciation for being alive, you realize that tension can be a reminder that you are alive. Every moment of life is precious and is a reason to celebrate the fact that you are alive.

Thinking is a reminder that your brain is working. Since your brain is working you can choose to say to yourself, "Right now, I am alive and I choose to release all stress and tension."

Stress and tension have many sources. There is the stress and tension of worry, of fear, of feeling nervous, or any kind of anxiety. Inner calm is the solution.

Let any form of needless stress remind you to create mental scenes that are conducive to being calm and relaxed. You might have a favorite serene scene, or you might enjoy creating new ones.

Tell your entire muscular system, "Muscles, relax." Hear your muscles responding, "Thank you for reminding me to loosen up and let go."

Since you are reading this in a present moment, right now, you can think about how you feel when you feel joyful. Then you can imagine how you will feel when you feel love for our Creator ("I love You, Hashem *Yisbarach*") and love for kindness. Then you can choose between thinking of upgrading your courage or upgrading your patience and serenity. You can even choose both thoughts.

> A fellow I know told me, "I used to be pretty calm. But as I am growing older I feel more of a constant rush to accomplish and achieve before it's too late. I know that it's healthier to be calm. My blood pressure tends to be high. And constantly being in a rush creates tension in my house. My frustration at not doing more causes me to lose my temper and speak in ways that I regret. What can I do about it?"
>
> I told him that he would benefit if he practiced releasing all tension and stress. He should tell his muscles to let go.
>
> "But how do I do it?" he asked. "It is too abstract for me."
>
> I shared the example that a coach I knew used: Hold a small object and release it, with your hand facing down.

"That is what releasing and letting go means. Since you open and close your hand many times each day, you take it for granted that you can do it. Letting go and releasing tension in all your other muscles is also easy once you realize that you can loosen all your muscles.

"So right now, tell your muscles what to do. Now, I let my jaw muscles relax. Now, I let my neck muscles relax. Now, I let my forehead muscles relax. Now, I let my arm muscles relax. Now, I let all my muscles from head to toe relax and let go.

"When you talk to yourself, speak in a calm and relaxing tone. Think about how people talk gently to infants when they want them to relax and fall asleep. The infant doesn't understand the words. But the infant is very attuned to the gentle energy. Try talking to your own muscles in a soothing voice. Each time you successfully do this, you will build up your mastery of being able to relax your muscles whenever you wish."

Joy made easy: the nine principles for happiness and joy for individuals and groups

Every time you think about happiness and joy in a positive way you improve yourself in ways that are consistent with happiness and joy.

I have found nine principles to be the cornerstone of the emotional base of people who have mastered happiness. At the top of the list is gratitude and kindness.

The Torah (*Devarim* 26:11) states, "Rejoice with all the good that the Almighty has given you." This is the Torah verse that tells us to be grateful for all that we have been given by the Creator.

In *Mishlei* (*Proverbs*) 15:15, King Solomon tells us, "Every day in the life of a poor person [that is, someone who keeps thinking about what is wrong and missing] is bad, but a person with a *tov lev*, a cheerful heart [that is, someone who is constantly grateful for the good in his life], will live life with the joy of a party." I have translated the verse here in accordance with the interpretation of the Vilna Gaon. At every moment, we choose whether to live with the distress of the first half of the verse, or whether we will joyfully experience life as expressed in the second half of the verse.

Individuals who regularly read these nine principles find that their minds automatically create more moments of happiness. An elaboration of this list can be found in my book, *Conversations with Yourself* (ArtScroll), Chapter 21.

Test it out for yourself. For the next 30 days read this list at least three times a day.

1. I think appreciatively and gratefully. What five things am I grateful for now?
2. I speak and act joyfully and kindly. (*When you speak and act joyfully and kindly, your brain produces the biochemicals that create joyful feelings.*)
3. I assume there is a benefit. What's good about this? (*Develop the skill of reframing. Find positive ways of viewing events, situations, and circumstances.*)
4. I strive for meaningful goals. What's my goal for now? (*Being clear about your priorities is the first step to accomplishing and achieving goals. Take a step forward.*)
5. I see myself being the way I wish to be. How do I want to be? (*As you picture yourself speaking and acting in ways consistent with your highest and wisest self, you create your ideal self.*)
6. I focus on solutions. What outcome am I looking for? (*If a problem arises, first clarify the problem. Then ask, "What can I do now to solve it?"*)
7. I let challenges develop my character. "This too will develop my character." (*Look at difficulties as Divinely sent opportunities to upgrade who you are. What quality can you develop now with a challenge that you faced or are facing now?*)
8. I consistently access positive states. My awesome brain stores my best states. What state do I want for right now?
   (*When you give names to your favorite and best moments, you*

will find them easier to access. Just tell your brain to access the specific state you want to experience now.)
9. I smile and wave to mirrors. They always smile and wave back to me. (*Research has shown that smiling to yourself in a mirror creates positive chemicals in your body. If you have a mirror handy, test your mirror to see if it will smile and wave to you when you smile and wave to it. This works even if you smile without a mirror.*)

Read these principles or recite them from memory a number of times a day. Reading them joyfully will create a few moments of joy whenever you wish. The more frequently and enthusiastically you review these ideas, the greater the imprint on your brain. Ultimately, that will mean many more moments of happiness and joy.

The positive effect is stronger when you read this list with a friend or group of friends. In a group, having discussions about these ideas will benefit all those who attend. Each individual will have a unique way of thinking and reacting. Those who learn from everyone will be able to learn a lot.

> *Someone who wanted to start a Happiness/Joy Club asked me for suggestions. He was just beginning his study of happiness and was very enthusiastic about developing himself with a group of people.*
>
> *I enthusiastically encouraged him. I shared what I learned from my experience of hosting the Joy Club of Jerusalem. Some of those ideas are scattered throughout this book.*
>
> *In Happiness or Joy Clubs, anyone can contribute helpful ideas, but everyone is also free to listen without commenting. Keep in mind that a Happiness/Joy Club is for increasing happiness and joy. The focus is on what to do to increase personal moments of happiness and joy.*

Focusing on what's wrong and what's missing

People who excel at focusing on what's wrong and what's missing in their lives also excel at making their lives totally miserable.

Yes, sometimes it is best to focus on what's wrong and to do what we can to fix it.

But it would be a big mistake to make finding problems the major theme of your personal life. Professionally, to earn money, you might be able to help people fix what is wrong and attain what is missing. But this should not be your major focus emotionally if you wish to live a meaningful, spiritual, joyful life.

To create more happy and joyful moments in your life, you need to keep your main focus on what you feel good about right now. By focusing on gratitude, you feel great love for our Creator, Who is the Source of all that you have. By focusing on gratitude to everyone who has helped you until the present moment, you feel greater love and appreciation for all the many people who have benefited you in some way.

This one change of focus creates consistent happiness for people who have previously created consistent unhappiness for themselves.

When you feel happy or joyful, ask yourself, *What am I focusing on right now that is giving me these good feelings?* The more time you spend focusing on similar patterns, the more time you will spend feeling happy and joyful.

When you feel unhappy, ask yourself, *What am I focusing on right now that is causing me these distressful feelings?* The less time you spend on similar patterns of focus, the more time you will feel happy.

Fully understanding that your focus creates your emotional state, for better or for worse, is one of the most important lessons we can learn. Teaching this by example to your children, students, friends, and anyone else you encounter will ensure that you are a consistently positive influence on the lives of others.

Knowing that you are an inspiration to other people is a tremendously positive source of spiritually meaningful good feelings.

> *In my "Four for Self-Creation" workshops, I focus on four key qualities: Happiness and Joy; Courage and Confidence; Love for Hashem and Love for people; and Serenity and Peace of mind. There are four major factors that create our lives: Self-talk, Self-image, Goals, Traits and States.*
>
> *A participant asked, "Could you give us a one-word summary of the key message?"*
>
> *"The word would be 'focus.' What you focus on creates your present experience of reality. Focus on negative self-talk, and you will feel distress and misery. Focus on happiness and joy in your self-talk, and that is how you will feel.*
>
> *"Focus on having low self-esteem and a negative self-image, and you create limitations and all the drawbacks of a negative sense of self. Focus on building your self-image and how you are created in the image of the Creator and*

Sustainer of the universe, and you build self-respect and a strong awareness of your immense self-worth.

"Focus on reaching your goals and you will reach them. Focus on the positive traits and states that you want for yourself, like Courage and Confidence, Kindness and Compassion, Serenity and Peace of Mind, and you will experience these ways of being more and more frequently."

After the workshop, one participant said to me, "That one word, 'Focus,' really worked for me. All of a sudden I realized that I didn't need to make my journey of self-development more complicated than necessary. I just have to remember, 'Focus,' and then I ask myself, 'What do I really want to focus on now?'

"I see how this will truly transform my life."

The art and skill of creating more moments of joy

When I give classes and workshops on how to create more moments of joy, I frequently start off by asking the participants: "Are you ready to create more moments of joy in your life?"

Those who are ready respond with a loud and enthusiastic, "Yes."

Perhaps you too are ready now. And if you aren't ready yet, you can decide to be ready at any moment. That moment will be a great moment in your life.

Consciously choosing to willfully add moments of joy to your life will benefit you for the rest of your life. You have a lot to gain and nothing to lose. The art and skill of creating more moments of joy is a fairly easy skill to learn. It took longer to learn many of your other skills!

Rambam (Maimonides) writes that the way to develop any trait is to practice the actions of that trait over and over again (*Hilchos Dei'os*, Ch. 1). That is the way to develop kindness, courage, patience, speaking and acting with joy, and gratitude. That is the way to become a person who takes action. (See *Yad Hachazakah, Hilchos Dei'os*, Chs. 1 and 2.)

Many people feel that they need special achievements and special occasions to experience joy. But we can all experience many moments of joy throughout a regular day. Allow this book to be your guide.

When you know how to create and access more joy, you will create a better life for yourself and your family. When you are in a joyful state, it's easier to be at your best. Being joyful is good for your health. Being joyful is conducive for getting along better with other people. Being joyful is at the root of authentic spirituality.

A person experiencing difficult and challenging life situations won't be happy. But he can still choose to say and do many things that will enable him to experience moments of joy. For example, a person who just lost his job isn't happy about it. He has a mortgage and is worried about how he will make the payments. But while he is thinking about what he can do to support his family and make the payments, he can still take actions that will be a source of meaningful joy. He can help a young child cross a busy street, or he can encourage someone who needs an emotional lift.

When a person makes a blessing before and after eating, he can be joyful that he is connecting with the Infinite and Eternal. He will still need to find solutions to his problems, but the moment of joy will put him in a better frame of mind for thinking more clearly.

A person who finds himself in a challenging environment is likely to find it difficult to maintain happiness. But he will still be able to create moments of joy throughout each day.

Moments of joy add up. The more joyful moments you experience, the easier it will be to create even more moments of joy. And when you think about your life, these moments of joy will automatically come to your mind.

A fellow who was in therapy for a long time came to one of my classes on joy.

After the class he told me a little about himself and mentioned, "I have been struggling with unhappiness and anger for a very long time. I have been trying to understand why I am the way I am. I have made a lot of progress but I am still very unhappy much of the time."

"How much time have you spent on creating more joy through gratitude, kindness, and meaningful goals?" I asked.

He responded, "This is the first time I've been to a yeshivah. I'm in business and I don't consider myself very spiritual. My therapist was interested in why I'm not happy. He would ask me each session, 'What have you learned lately about the roots of your unhappiness?'"

"Would you really like to be joyful?" I asked him.

"I haven't thought too much about joy. I spend my time on building my business. When I do think about how I feel, I just relive the unhappy scenes and try to understand the roots of my unhappiness."

"Unhappiness can have many roots in the past. But in the present you're not using your mind the right way if you really want to be joyful. The way to create more joy is to spend more time thinking about gratitude. It's great that you came to our yeshivah. You will learn how to think and speak with greater gratitude. You will learn about engaging in more acts of kindness. And you will upgrade your life goals regardless of what you do financially. This is a proven recipe for increasing happiness," I explained.

"It makes sense to me," he responded.

"Realize that the idea of focusing for a long time on the opposite of happiness and joy in order to gain insight is a fairly new idea. That idea was not developed by studying the thoughts and actions of truly joyful people. Recent brain research is totally consistent with what Rambam (Maimonides) wrote about increasing the time you act consistent with the traits that you want to develop."

The special word that creates joy

Words are instructions for the mind. When you speak to someone else, the words you say create thoughts, pictures, and feelings in that person.

For English speakers, the word *tree* creates an image of an object that we call a tree. Someone might refer to a specific tree: an apple tree, an orange tree, or a coconut tree. As long as you recognize these words, you will have a different picture for each tree. Even if you don't see mental pictures easily, you will understand there are different types of trees.

The word *flower* also creates a picture. It could create a picture of a rose or a tulip, or even an entire garden of flowers. If you suggest that someone mentally picture the most beautiful garden imaginable, he will create a very different picture and feeling than if told to imagine a garbage dump.

The word *mountain* creates a different picture than the word *valley*. The word *rain* demands a different picture than the word *snow*. If you suggest that someone imagine a vacation at the Swiss Alps and how wonderful he would feel if actually there, the suggestion is likely to elicit a positive feeling.

Similarly, the words you say to yourself also serve as instructions for your brain and mind.

There is a special word that you can say to yourself that has the marvelous ability to create thoughts and feelings of joy. For English speakers, it is the word *joy*. Someone who wants to increase his experiences of joy should talk about being joyful more often.

When you see pictures of people, you can easily recognize who is joyful and who is sad. You have a mental image of the way a person who experiences joy will look.

You also know how someone who is authentically joyful will sound. If you listen to two recordings, you will easily be able to recognize the difference between a person who is clearly sad and a person who is clearly joyful.

Moreover, you know how you feel when you feel joyful and how you feel when you feel miserable.

If you have experienced joy many times in your life and someone asks you to think of joyful feelings, the word *joy* will elicit a feeling of joy.

If your feelings are associated with the words *unhappy, angry, upset, miserable, nervous, worried, resentful*, or *stuck*, you might not find it easy to feel the feelings associated with *joy*.

But if you have experienced many experiences of joy, and right now you are feeling calm and relaxed, most likely you will be able to feel good feelings when you are asked, "Could you please tell me in detail about some of your favorite joyful moments?"

A person who is able to access feelings of joy at will and frequently mentions the word *joy* will create a more joyful life.

It is possible to talk about joy and then feel bad for not feeling as much joy as you would wish. But this isn't necessary. You are in the process of learning the skill of experiencing more joy. You can feel good about having this as your goal.

The Almighty leads a person along the path that he wants to go.

(See Talmud, *Makkos* 10b.) Ask for Divine assistance in your quest for more joy. You will live a happier and healthier life. You will be able to help others be more joyful. And you will be more joyful when you pray and devote yourself to spiritual pursuits.

How often do you presently think and talk about being joyful? As you add the words *joy* and *joyful* to your everyday self-talk and when talking to others, you will find yourself being joyful much more frequently.

> *I recently spoke to a 30-year-old fellow who complained that he feels awful most of the time.*
>
> *"I don't know why I feel so bad," he said. "Nothing is really that wrong in my life. I have challenges like everybody else. While I'm not as successful now as I wish I were, I don't consider myself a failure. I'm wondering about the root of my unhappiness. Can you give me some insight into my situation?"*
>
> *"Would you like to be joyful?" I asked him.*
>
> *"I can't imagine myself being joyful," he said. "I just want to stop feeling bad. I'm not optimistic that someone like me could actually be joyful."*
>
> *"For the next few days, keep a journal of how you feel," I suggested. "Ask yourself, 'How do I feel now?' at least twenty times each day."*
>
> *Four days later he had his report neatly written. The words he used to describe his feelings were "depressed," "upset," "frustrated," "angry," "sad," and "resentful."*
>
> *I commented, "I noticed that you don't have 'joyful' written down even once. Why not?"*
>
> *"It's obvious why not," he said. "I told you that I didn't believe that I could be joyful."*
>
> *"I appreciate the way you dutifully carried out your assignment of writing down your feelings. Now, for the next week please say the word 'joyful' at least 25 times a day. I know that now it's difficult for you to feel joyful, but still make a sincere effort to say the word 'joyful' as joyfully as you can.*

"Mark down each time you say this. Let's see what happens."

The fellow followed through on his commitment. He had a smile on his face when he told me, "I didn't think that this would be helpful for me. But I'm glad that I'm mistaken. I felt so much better after the 25 times a day, that I used the word 'joy' many more times. It was an entirely new experience for me. I felt better this week than I have in a long while."

Focusing on joy is the key to being more joyful

Whatever you focus your attention on, you increase. This one principle is the key to mastering any trait and skill.

A person who focuses on building his self-image will eventually think like a person who has a positive self-image. He will feel like a person who has a positive self-image. He will speak and act the way a person with a positive self-image speaks and acts. I have elaborated on this in my book *Building Your Self-Image and the Self-Image of Others*.

A person whose goal is not to feel unhappy so much of the time will probably *increase* the amount of time he feels unhappy. That wasn't his intention, but unwittingly he is creating more of what he doesn't want.

Focus on what you *do* want. Make your goal explicit. "My goal is to increase my moments of joy." This way, every single moment of joy is a successful moment.

Celebrate each moment of joy. Be grateful every time you experience joy.

Having this goal will place your attention on joy. Instead of feeling bad when you are not joyful, you will experience positive feelings about experiencing more joy.

Each moment of joy in your entire life is experienced one moment at a time. You can't have more than one moment of joy in any given moment, but you can increase the number of joyful moments. How? By focusing on it.

Write this sentence in a place where you will easily see it: "Focusing on joy is the key to being more joyful."

Share this idea with others. Talk about it. If you write someone a letter or an e-mail, mention it.

I have found it amazing that people who have been unhappy for a very long time will make great progress in a relatively short time, by focusing on creating moments of joy.

Just as focusing on joy creates more joy, so too focusing on courage creates more courage. Similarly, focusing on love for Hashem and for kindness creates more love and kindness. And the same with serenity: focusing on being calmly serene will create greater inner calm. Focusing on being serenely empowered will enable you to be in this state more often.

> *An idealistic fellow said, "I want to be joyful all the time. How do I accomplish this seemingly impossible goal?"*
>
> *"I agree with you," I said to him. "This goal is an impossible goal. People who want to be joyful all the time can easily focus on their moments without joy. If one's goal is to 'always' be joyful, then every moment of lack of joy is a failure to meet this goal. Thinking about joy with this mind-set will increase your distress.*
>
> *"I suggest that you make a more modest goal. When your goal is just to experience joy more frequently, there is a good chance that you will succeed. And this will add to your joy.*

You will feel good that you feel good instead of feeling bad that you feel bad."

The fellow looked as if a great weight had been taken off his shoulders. He smiled and commented, "Thank you very much. I see that when I make my goal more reachable, I will find it so much easier to go in the direction that I really want to go."

Your Creator gave you an endorphin factory

When you experience joy, you feel good because your magnificent brain produces hormones called endorphins. These self-produced chemicals give you happy and joyful feelings.

Research on these biochemicals has proven that the brain-produced hormones enter your bloodstream even if you just act joyful, not only when you really are happy. Although the joyful experience is totally imaginary and you know that it didn't actually happen, when you speak and act as if that imaginary experience did happen, you get a dose of endorphins.

These chemicals are naturally produced by your brain. They are totally free and entirely healthy.

Many people find that this knowledge inspires them to create more joyful moments. It's not just an abstract idea, but a physical reality.

This knowledge is especially important when we are engaged in Torah, prayer, and acts of kindness. The ideal is to serve the Almighty with joy. A deep awareness of how awesome it is to fulfill the will of our Father, our King, Creator and Sustainer of the universe can fill our entire system with a profound level of joy.

Someone may not yet be at this joyful level of serving Hashem. If he can speak and act as though he experiences this spiritual awareness on an emotional level, his brain will produce endorphins.

These naturally produced chemicals are neurotransmitters and enhance our brain's functioning intellectually. We remember better, we think more clearly, and we are more creative with endorphins in our system.

When you smile, your brain produces endorphins. The more frequently you smile an authentic smile, the more frequently you increase your endorphin level. A friend of mine told me that when he smiled to the Creator when he prayed, his experience of praying was taken to a whole new level.

When taking a test, an increased endorphin level helps you do better than if you were in a more standard state. This is especially noteworthy, since it's normal to feel more tense and stressed when taking a test.

My daughter's late father-in-law Rabbi Avraham Baharan was a high school principal who had a clever school policy. His teachers had to promote laughter before giving tests. In his experience, the students invariably got higher grades when they were in a humorous state. Endorphins produced by laughter enable a student's brain to work at optimal level.

> *Someone once told me that he has a problem with overeating. He had to cut down on his sugar intake. But when he was nervous, he tended to binge on cookies, ice cream, and chocolate. It wasn't healthy and his physician warned him strongly that his eating habits were threatening his health.*
>
> *He told me that he unsuccessfully tried many methods to help him cut down on his eating. When he felt calm, he was able to be careful about what he ate. He had the self-discipline to resist the temptation to eat food that he liked*

but knew wasn't good for him. But when he was nervous, he found that eating sugary food calmed him down.

I suggested that he utilize the power of laughter to get an endorphin increase. He told me that he didn't find most jokes funny.

I told him that laughing produces endorphins, even if someone laughs because he decides to laugh, even if nothing is especially funny. So when he is nervous, instead of eating something sugary, he should develop the habit of laughing.

It might be easier to laugh if he remembers a time when he laughed and laughed and couldn't stop laughing. But even when he can't recall such spontaneous laughter, he could make himself laugh the way he did when he "really laughed."

It worked for him. Try it and see how it works for you.

Joy is created and stored in your brain

When you are joyful, your brain has created that joy. You might think that an external event or situation caused that joy, and may seek joy from something external. Thinking that joy is found only outside of you will prevent you from using the full potential of your mind. Yes, external events and situations can be a catalyst. But it is always in your own brain and mind that joy is created.

Every joyful moment of your life is stored in your brain. If you don't recall a specific joyful moment, you might not access it to experience it again. However, that moment *is* stored in your brain. Memories of what you saw, heard, and felt when you were joyful are all stored in your brain.

Some people find it easy to relive their joyful moments. They can easily experience those moments again and again. They are fortunate.

Many other people are masters at feeling bad. They find it very easy to recall the distressful and negative events that happened to them. They live that same distress over and over again. This pattern can be a source of much misery. However, these people can also learn to become masters at recalling moments of joy.

Since you are reading this book, I assume that you would prefer to be a master at recalling joyful moments.

Right now tell yourself, *My goal is to be a master at recalling my positive and meaningful joyful moments.*

Point to your head and say to yourself, *Every moment of joy that I have ever experienced throughout my life is stored in my amazing brain.*

Your personal archives and library of joyful moments are stored in your portable G-d-given mental computer. So are your moments of courage, serenity, love for the Creator, and love for kindness.

Knowing that your mind can access the memories of joy and other positive traits makes the entire process of being more joyful much easier.

Just knowing this piece of information is insufficient, however. We must draw our mind's attention to the joy that is already stored within.

As you continue to read this book and apply the exercises, you will gain a greater awareness of what you can do to improve your skill of creating more moments of joy, courage, love, and serenity.

> *I had spoken to someone a number of times about accessing joy more often. He didn't really grasp how joyful moments were stored in his brain.*
>
> *"I was told as a child that it's difficult to be joyful," he said to me. "Life is hard, I was told, and only a small minority of people really have a great life. As I got older I saw that they were right. So many things go wrong in life. There are many disappointments. There are moments of celebration every now and then. But it's unrealistic to expect to be joyful most of the time," he concluded.*
>
> *He had recently bought a new computer and was very excited about the possibilities it gave him.*
>
> *"The portable computer that the Creator gave you is much*

more powerful," I told him. "You have every moment of joy that you ever experienced stored in your brain. To access those feelings, you don't need to push any buttons. You only need to focus on 'joyful moments that I've already experienced.'"

"I don't know if I'll actually be able to do this," he timidly said.

"Every single person who ever lived is able to do this. Some people realize that they can do this, and some people don't yet realize it. Just as everyone can feel bad a large number of times over something that already happened in the past, so too everyone can feel good over and over again by remembering joyful moments."

The fellow wasn't certain that what I said would apply to him.

I told him, "Right now when you are thinking about whether or not you can do this, you are not practicing. You are just contemplating whether you can or you can't. By actually trying to access the joyful memories, you will have real experiences. As you focus on applying this, you will experientially know that you are able to do it. Be patient. And be open to experiment."

He calmed down and reported that it was so much easier than he had imagined. "It's amazing that such a simple practice can make such a major difference in my life."

Send joyful energy to your brain, heart, lungs, throat, tongue, etc.

How do you lift up your hands? Your brain sends energy to your arms and hands and you are able to lift them.

How do you walk? Your brain sends energy down to your feet and your feet move and carry your mind along for the journey.

How do you talk? Your brain sends energy to your mouth and tongue and they make the sounds that your mind chooses.

The process of sending energy from your brain to various parts of your body happens the entire day, every day.

Similarly, you can send joyful energy to every part of your body that your mind chooses. Joyful energy is healthy for your entire physical structure and everything within.

Just as we can't explain with words how we send energy to our hands and to our feet, so too we can't explain verbally how we send joyful energy to any part of ourselves. The important thing is that we know we can do this.

Right now say to yourself joyfully, *Now, I am going to send joyful energy to my brain.*

Then you can say, *Now, I am going to send joyful energy to my heart.*

Then, *Now, I am going to send joyful energy to my lungs.*

Then, *Now, I am going to send joyful energy to my throat.*

One by one, send joyful energy to your kidneys, to your stomach, to your neck, to your eyes, to your ears, to your forehead, to your fingers and your hands, and to your toes and your feet.

After doing this a number of times, your brain will have been trained to send joyful energy to specific areas of your body. So you will be able to streamline the process by saying: *Right now, my brain will send joyful energy to my entire body from head to toe.*

When you feel especially joyful, utilize the experience to build up the power of this suggestion. Again, it's: *Right now, my brain will send joyful energy to my entire body from head to toe.*

This can be especially beneficial for individuals who experience a lot of stress. When you send joy along your nerves and muscles, nervousness melts away and positive, healing energy takes its place.

> *I shared this section with someone, but he told me, "This idea is too abstract for me. I feel awful so much of the time that this suggestion won't work for me."*
>
> *When a person has a strong belief that something will not work, his mind will do what it can to prove him right.*
>
> *So I suggested a way to make it more tangible. "First repeat the word 'JOY!!!' joyfully, a number of times. Say this as enthusiastically as you can. When you feel even a little better than usual, place the palm of your hand (either right or left) on your forehead and say, 'I now send joyful energy from my hand to my forehead.'*
>
> *"Then place your right hand over your right eye and your left hand over your left eye, and say, 'I now send joyful energy from my hands to my eyes.'*

"Then place your hands over your ears and say, 'I now send joyful energy from my hands to my ears.'

"Then place one hand around the front of your neck and the other hand around the back and say, 'I now send joyful energy to my neck and throat.'

"Then put your right hand on your left shoulder and say, 'I now send joyful energy to my shoulder.' Repeat with your left hand on your right shoulder.

"Don't expect to feel extremely great. Look for moments of improvement. After experimenting with this for a while and finding that it's becoming effective, you will find it easier to send joyful energy with your mind and speech alone."

29

The most joyful feeling in the world

The most joyful feeling in the world is the awareness that your Father, your King, the Creator and Sustainer of the universe, is lovingly giving you the greatest gift possible: life this very moment. What a great consciousness! It's awesome.

Someone told me, "I was feeling needlessly unhappy much too often. I was frequently disappointed with my life. I had high aspirations and while I did accomplish a bit, it was a far cry from what I was hoping for.

"And then I read a quote that you cited from the Chazon Ish (Emunah U'Bitachon 1:9) in your book, My Father, My King: Connecting with the Creator. *'When a person merits becoming aware of the reality of the Almighty's existence, he will experience limitless joy. All the pleasures of the flesh immediately disappear. His soul is enveloped in sanctity and it is as if it has left the body and floats in the upper Heavens. When a person transcends to this level, an entire new world is open to him. All of the*

pleasures of this world are as nothing compared to the intense pleasure of a person cleaving to his Creator.'

"This thought opened up my mind to the great opportunity for emotional elevation that I could have through increased spirituality. Even though I knew that this wasn't a level that an ordinary person like myself could attain on a regular basis, it was still a spark of insight and inspiration. I felt as if I had turned a corner in my life.

"I would say to Hashem a number of times a day, 'Hashem, I thank You for giving me life right now. I love You with all my heart and all my soul, to the best of my ability right this moment. I wish to serve You with joy and love. Bless me with the pleasure of my soul cleaving to You. Let me love You and love people. Let me bring joy to You and joy to other people.'

"This short prayer lifted my spirits when I was down and increased my good feelings when I was up. I suggest that other people compose their own prayer, or they can write down mine. It's a gift to anyone who hears it."

If I were a master of joy, how would I speak and act now?

When you want to access a joyful state, ask yourself, *If I were a master of joy, how would I speak and act now?*

Since this method doesn't ask you to feel anything you're not actually feeling, it will be easier to speak and act the way you would if were a master of joy. This is the power of acting "as if."

I have found that people who once claimed, "I can't just decide to be joyful when I don't really feel joyful," were able to benefit from this approach.

This same principle applies when you choose to speak and act as if you were fearless and courageous. You are likely to find that you can say and do things that would usually be difficult for you to say and do. Even though you might not view yourself as a fearless person, you can still choose to speak and act fearless in any given situation. So keep in mind the question, "If I were totally fearless, what would I be able to say and do right now?"

You can choose to speak and act as if you were a master of serenity. Ask yourself, *If I were a master of serenity, how would I speak and act right now?*

The more frequently you practice this approach, the more you will integrate and internalize speaking and acting the way you would if you were joyful, courageous, and serene. Eventually, you won't need to make a special effort to speak and act this way. It will become automatic and natural.

> *A highly intelligent, accomplished gentleman came to a class that I gave. After the class, he said to me, "When you spoke about becoming a more joyful person, it really hit home. I have every reason to be grateful and happy, but I'm not. I always think about how much more I need to do to feel positive about myself.*
>
> *"It's not that I have a low self-image. As a matter of fact, my self-image is really very high. That is exactly the source of my frequent feelings of frustration. I know that I have accomplished a lot. But if I utilized more of my potential I would achieve a lot more."*
>
> *I responded, "It seems that you believe that you need to accomplish all that you can before you allow yourself to experience consistent joy. That's a mistake. Right at this moment you can choose to experience joy."*
>
> *"But how can I be joyful? I'm not accomplishing all that I can accomplish."*
>
> *"The only day you can say that you accomplished all that you can accomplish is on the last day of your life on this planet. As long as the Almighty gives you life, He is giving you a message that you still can accomplish more.*
>
> *"Right now you are still alive. Right now you have free will to choose how you will think, feel, speak, and act. I would like to suggest a powerful tool.*
>
> *"Each day, ask yourself, 'If I were a master of joy, what would I think, feel, say, and do?'*

"You might never totally master being joyful. But don't let that stop you from thinking, feeling, speaking, and acting like a master of joy."

"I have to be honest about it. I'm not a master of joy," he insisted.

"I realize that you haven't mastered joy yet. And we don't know now if you ever will. But even so you can choose to love yourself. The Almighty loves you. So choose to love what the Almighty loves. And choose to think, feel, speak, and act like a master of joy. When you do, you will certainly be more joyful than you are now."

What a group of 2-year-olds taught me about joy

I have given a number of "Joy Workshops" to a group of 2-year-old children. I have given them moments of joy. In return I learned a great lesson about creating moments of joy.

A niece of mine runs a private *gan* (playgroup) for 2-year-old toddlers. My daughter's family lives down the block, so I drop by the *gan* regularly.

When I was beginning to write this book, I thought it would be a good idea to teach the word "joy" to the little kids attending the *gan*. So I smiled and waved to the toddlers, who reminded me of my grandchildren, and joyfully said, "Joy."

I repeated the word "joy" for around 15 seconds. Then I waved and said, "Bye-bye."

The next time I came to the house when the *gan* was in session, I repeated the ritual of the last time.

Some of the more outgoing children repeated the word "joy" and smiled.

The next time even more children reacted joyfully and repeated the word.

The time after that, every little child came to the door and joyfully said, "Joy."

I did this about once a week. After a while, as soon as I knocked on the door, the children would chant, "Joy."

I tremendously enjoyed this experience, and so did anyone who heard the story.

Upon reflection, I realized that these small children are totally in the present. Not one of them thinks, *How can I be joyful now? When I go home, my older brother or sister might take away a toy I want to play with. My mother might not give me my favorite food. I might fall down and start crying.*

They were totally in the present moment. When they heard me say, "Joy," they gleefully followed my example. There was not one bit of resistance to being joyful during that moment.

Every person who reads this was once a 2-year-old child. You, too, could have easily been joyful when someone joyfully said, "Joy," to you.

You still can do this now, in the present. Picture yourself as a happy toddler. Imagine that you are attending a "Joy Workshop." Imagine that all you need to do is joyfully repeat the word "joy" and you will experience a moment of joy.

> *A highly pessimistic middle-aged man told me that he finds it very difficult to be happy. He has experienced so much negativity in his life that when he thinks of the future, he immediately assumes that he will experience more of the same.*
>
> *"I have no way of knowing how your future will unfold," I said. "But one thing I am certain of. If you keep up your pattern of thinking and talking in such a depressingly unhappy way, you will not be creating moments of joy." I shared with him my experience with the group of 2-year-olds.*
>
> *"I would like to give you some homework. Each day for*

two whole minutes, imagine that you are once again 2 years old. Now, as an adult, speak to your little 2-year-old self and joyfully repeat the word 'joy.' At first this will probably be difficult for you to do. You will argue that this doesn't seem natural to you. You will argue that this is not who you are. You will even argue that this won't work.

"Stop arguing. Start experimenting. Three times a day for an entire week, spend two minutes repeating the word 'joy' joyfully while looking at yourself in a mirror. Do this when no one is around so you won't be too self-conscious. Use all your willpower and actually do this three times a day. I'm certain it will work if you give it a sincere try."

He did, and he had to admit that it did work.

Will it work for you? My guess is that it will. The only question is whether you will be playful enough to test it out for yourself. As you do this experiment, put any pessimistic tendencies aside for the two minutes needed, three times a day. A six-minute-a-day investment of time is well worth the multitude of benefits of increasing your level of joy.

Persist to master joy

Persistence is the quality that helps people succeed.
Quitting prevents people from reaching their goals. Many realistic goals aren't reached because the person who made them stopped too soon.

We have the invention of lightbulbs because their inventor kept trying until he succeeded. Every time you see a lightbulb, you have another reminder of the tremendous power of persistence.

When your goal is to master being more joyful, you have a great advantage over Edison. Edison had no guarantee that his persistence would create a successful lightbulb. However, when you make it your goal to increase your moments of joy, you will definitely be successful. It's not just a "maybe."

Be patient. Patience is the key to persistence.

Sometimes it can be very challenging to be patient. If it were an easy trait to master, everyone would be patient.

We find it relatively easy to be patient when we enjoy what we are doing. We are also more patient when we recognize the vast benefits of being persistent. If you feel that you have little to gain, you probably won't be as patient as when you know that the benefits will be magnificent.

You will gain tremendously by increasing your moments of joy (and courage, and serenity, and kindness). Be patient. Read this entire book, because you don't know which idea will be most beneficial.

Review this book a number of times. Each time you read it, you will gain a greater awareness of what to do to gain greater mastery over your mind and your life.

> *A fellow I spoke to about improving his life said to me, "I know that a lot of ideas you have told me will be good for me. When I try out some of the exercises, I do gain. But I guess that I lack patience.*
>
> *"I've always been impatient. My parents and teachers often told me that I need to be more patient. But what can I do? I'm missing patience. I know it would be great if I were blessed with more patience. But I'm just not patient."*
>
> *"The way you are looking at patience isn't helpful and it isn't reality," I told him. "You look at patience as something that some people have more of and some people have less.*
>
> *"But that's not the way it is. Patience is a trait that everyone can build up. When you do something many times, it increases your level of patience. You don't have a finite amount and it can't get used up. Rather, patience consists of actions that you can choose to do.*
>
> *"Let's take the trait of being joyful. Many actions of joy will increase the amount of joy that is stored in your brain. Being patient and persistent just means that you will keep up the practice of speaking and acting joyfully.*
>
> *"If you were patient and persisted about increasing joy, how many times a day would you like to joyfully say the word 'joyful'?"*
>
> *He committed to a number.*
>
> *I told him that I would hold him accountable to his commitment. He should mark down each time he joyful says the*

word "joyfully." He proved to himself that he was able to be more persistent than he had originally thought.

How many times a day would you like to commit to repeating the word "joy"? It will be helpful to ask a friend to make sure that you are following through on your commitment.

This will work best if you find someone with a similar goal. You can then regularly ask each other if you met your day's quota.

33

The self-talk of joy

As you are reading this, you are also engaging in self-talk. If you are thinking, *I like this point*, that is self-talk. Thinking, *I don't get it*, or *I disagree with this*, is self-talk, too.

People create more joy with self-talk that is conducive to joy. People create and enhance their negative feelings with negative self-talk.

Fortunately, you create your self-talk. In my book *Conversations with Yourself,* I elaborated on the topic of self-talk, but I summarize the key points below.

You are always in the present. And in the present your mind is always thinking of something. This thinking can also be considered self-talk.

You get to choose your self-talk each and every moment of your life.

When your self-talk is conducive to feeling sad or nervous or angry or worried or fearful, you won't be feeling joyful.

When your self-talk is focused on all the many things you appreciate and are grateful for in your life, in the present and in the past, you will feel happier and more joyful.

Some people are more aware of their constant flow of self-talk and some are less aware. To be joyful, gain greater awareness of what you are saying in the inner recesses of your mind. If you are not yet flowing with joyful self-talk, make it a priority to upgrade your self-talk.

"Upgrade your self-talk and you upgrade your life." This is the motto that I have on my index cards. I personally appreciate reminders. I need it. If you are reading this book to help you increase your joyful moments, I suggest that you keep reminding yourself of this mental principle.

Frequently say this self-talk sentence to yourself: *Each time I talk to myself about increasing my joyful self-talk, I increase my moments of joy.*

You become more of an expert at what you keep practicing. As you keep practicing joyful self-talk, it becomes easier and easier.

The same applies to self-talk about all the other positive qualities you want for yourself. The more you hear your self-talk of serenity, courage, kindness, and compassion, the more serene, courageous, and kind you will become. The more you practice self-talk about joyfully making and reaching goals, the more proficiently you will joyfully make and reach goals.

> *"It's not my fault that I am unhappy so much of the time," someone said to me. "I had an unhappy childhood. Both my parents were unhappy a lot of the time. I had awful role models."*
>
> *"Of course you shouldn't blame yourself for your unhappiness," I agreed. "You are a sensible and rational human being and you would prefer to be happy. You dream of being successful in life. You feel that success will make you happy.*
>
> *"But what will really make you happy is upgrading your self-talk. You don't need to wait until you reach your definition of super success. You have the free will to choose joyful self-talk right this moment.*

"I agree that having a joyful childhood and joyful parents as role models makes it much easier to have joyful self-talk. But you are responsible for your choices now. And in the present, you have the ability to choose joyful self-talk."

He asked, "But if things are going roughly for me, isn't it dishonest to talk to myself as if I were successful?"

"We pray each day for wisdom. We need a wise balance to choose self-talk that is honest and conducive to positive self-development. You have a lot to be grateful for in the present, even though you wish things were easier and better for you. But this doesn't need to prevent you from becoming a master of positive and wise self-talk.

"Don't waste your time and energy on feeling bad that you feel bad. Focus on improving your self-talk. As you improve your inner world of thoughts and feelings, you will find yourself making wiser choices.

"Right now, reflect on how much better your life will be when you gain greater mastery over your self-talk."

He reported that every time he engaged in more upbeat self-talk, he really did feel much better. You will also when you patiently develop this pattern.

Determination to be joyful today will enable you to create a more joyful day

Determination is a strong will to use your skills and talents to reach a specific goal. In Hebrew this is called *ratzon*.

There is an often-quoted saying, "Nothing stands in the way of a strong *ratzon*." This is based on the Talmudic statement (*Makkos* 10b) that the Almighty will lead us on a path when we have a strong will for that path.

We live one day at a time. To make joy easier to attain, decide to be joyful just for today. Tomorrow you can be determined to make that day joyful. But today you only need to decide for today.

Everyone would like to be joyful, but not everyone is willing to do all that they could to actually create daily joy. In general, the more determined you are to reach a goal, the more time and effort you are willing to invest. Since you are reading this book, you are already showing a strong interest in increasing your joy.

Some people argue, "I'm just not the determined type. I start many things but don't follow through. If something seems like too much effort, I give up right at the beginning."

When something is truly important to you, you will have much more determination than usual. This is especially true when you greatly enjoy doing what you are determined to do.

Think about times when you have been very determined. You might have been determined to buy something that was difficult to get. It might not have been truly important in the scheme of things, but you persevered. You made the necessary telephone calls. You went places. You didn't give up until you got what you wanted.

Every young child is extremely determined throughout his childhood. For example, as a young child, you were determined to walk. Therefore the quality of determination is already stored in your brain. Now you can apply this quality in your quest for increased joy in your life.

> "It's just not working," someone complained to me. "I really and truly want to live a happier life, but I'm far from the way I would like to be. I have given up many times. Every once in a while I try again, but it seems I'm doing something wrong. What can I do differently to be more successful at becoming a more joyful person?"
>
> "Can you please list some examples of goals that you successfully reached?" I asked him.
>
> He rattled off a number of things.
>
> "What is the difference in the way you went about the task of striving for the goals that you successfully reached and the goals that you didn't?"
>
> At first the fellow couldn't answer the question. But I assured him that he could take his time and really think the matter through carefully.
>
> "There must be a major distinction," I said to him. "When you are aware of the different approaches, you will gain

insight into what enabled you to be successful."

He thought the matter over carefully. "I think I got it," he said. "When I was truly determined to do whatever it would take, I succeeded. When I wasn't successful, it was because I wasn't as committed. Because I wasn't so strongly determined, I cut corners. I tried to take the easy way out. I mentally gave up even though I still went through the motions."

"What one word would you use to describe the difference?" I asked him.

"Determination!" he replied.

"There is no comparison between the way I thought and felt when I was truly determined, and when I lacked determination. Now that you helped point it out to me, I can see how I was like a totally different person when I was determined to succeed.

"I now realize that if I am totally determined to master joy, I will do all that is in my power to become joyful."

This fellow became totally determined to become more joyful and he was successful. Will you follow his example?

You are alive! Therefore you have a reason to be joyful

When I suggest that people choose to be joyful in any present moment, some people argue, "If nothing special is happening, how can I just choose to be joyful? It won't be real joy."

People who win a major lottery prize are able to celebrate because they think this prize will give them happiness. Being alive is the ultimate thing to celebrate. As long as you are alive, so many options are open to you.

Developing the ability to choose to be joyful just because you are alive is a skill like any other skill. When you practice enough times, you will experience it on a biochemical and neurological level.

Think about what it would be like to celebrate joyously. How would you sound? What would you say? What would you look like?

You may start to celebrate being alive only to see if you can make this work. But when you go through the right motions, you will eventually be able to truly celebrate at will.

To make this celebration of life seem more authentic, exclaim as if you were experiencing great joy, "I am celebrating that I am alive." Keep repeating this with the most joyful tone of voice that you've ever heard. Move your hands and arms the way people do in a great celebration. Do it over and over again while saying, "The greatest thing that I could ever experience is being alive, and I am alive now."

It's normal for people to just argue, "I can't do this. It's silly." It might be a bit silly, but if you actually go through the motions correctly, it works.

If someone wants to prove he *can't* do it, he will successfully block this joyful celebration of life. But if someone will invest enough time and honestly make the effort, he will see that he can learn this skill.

To upgrade your joyful celebration of life, shout with great excitement, "Right now I am alive! And because I am alive I can choose Joy, Courage, Love ("I love You, Hashem *Yisbarach*"), and Serenity."

People have repeated these exercises with great enthusiasm and actually felt the words having a positive effect on them. They have found that it was well worth the effort.

> *I shared this idea in a class and one fellow kept arguing that there was no way that this would actually work for him.*
>
> *Someone else in the room disagreed. He said, "I, too, used to think that I wouldn't be able to do this. But someone made an offer that I couldn't refuse. He told me to imagine that I was going to be paid a huge amount of money to play this role in a professional production. I was to play the role of a person who could rejoice about being alive whenever I chose to.*
>
> *"Well, I had to admit that if someone would offer me a fortune for acting this part in a play, I probably would be able to do it. I would take a few acting lessons and learn how. But*

the fellow insisted that I imagine I had already taken the acting lessons, and now was going to prove that I could do it. I laughed and was able to imagine myself doing it. That made me more open to practice."

The person in our class stopped arguing. He realized that he too would be able to do it if he kept practicing.

Count joyfully

Every time you need to routinely count anything, you have an opportunity to add sparks of joy into your present moment by habitually counting this way:

"1-Joy!"
"2-Joy!"
"3-Joy!"
"4-Joy!"
"5-Joy!"
"6-Joy!"
"7-Joy!"
"8-Joy!"
"9-Joy!"
"10-Joy!"

It will take longer than if you just counted without saying, "Joy!" But it will routinely add good feelings into your life, so it's usually worth the time investment of the seconds it takes to count this way. Imagine how wonderful it will be for the quality of your life if you make this way of counting a habit.

Of course, if you must count quickly, don't count this way.

When you make it a habit to count, "1-Joy! 2-Joy! 3-Joy! 4-Joy!," etc., your brain will automatically associate your counting with the feelings connected to the word "Joy!"

If you begin to feel impatient while waiting on line and you aren't already thinking of something especially constructive, utilize this opportunity to create more moments of joy by counting joyfully.

For people who find it difficult to "Joy Count," I recommend that they "Joy Count" from 1 to 100 with a few friends. The energy of more people makes it easier and more effective.

If someone finds it very difficult to be joyful for a few moments, I recommend that he meet with a group of at least 10 people (an entire *minyan*) and "Joy Count" from 1 to 1000. For this to work properly, every participant should "Joy Count" with as much energy and intensity as he can. The more energy and intensity they use when counting, the more powerful the effect. When they reach "1,000-JOY!" they can celebrate a great victory.

> *A student told me that he has a problem with being very impatient. This causes him much frustration on a daily level when he has to wait for family members. He loses his temper when interacting with his children, when their only offense is acting the way children normally act when they are tired or hungry.*
>
> *I suggested that he practice counting "1-Joy, 2-Joy, 3-Joy" and so on, to enable himself to access a better state.*
>
> *I advised him to begin by practicing "Joyful Counting" when he was feeling O.K. If he were naturally joyful about something, that would be an even more effective time to practice. The joyful feelings would be associated with the joyful counting. But even if he didn't get a chance to "Joy Count" before he needed it the most, he could begin to "Joy Count" when he needed to become calmer and think more clearly.*
>
> *Two days later he called to tell me that he was pleasantly surprised by how easy and beneficial he found "Joy Counting."*

I am joyfully grateful for each and every breath

As you read this sentence, you are breathing. Throughout the entire day today you will be breathing.

The Sages have taught us to be grateful for each and every breath. This is based on the last verse of *Tehillim* (*Psalms*) that says our entire soul should praise the Almighty. The Hebrew word for soul is *neshamah,* which is similar to the Hebrew word *neshimah,* breath.

The more frequently you focus on your appreciation and gratitude for each breath, the greater will be your sense of daily gratitude. You can easily add the word "joy" into your new habitual practice.

Since every breath you take is always in the present moment, focusing on gratitude for a breath will also focus your mind on the present moment. This is especially important when you are worrying about the future or being upset about something in the past.

Right now you are still breathing. Great! Now say, "I am joyfully grateful for each and every breath."

People who focus on their slow and deep breathing as a daily practice find that this enables them to be calmer and more serene. Research has shown that when someone breathes this way for 20 minutes, the entire mind-body has "the relaxation response." This is the exact opposite of entering "the fight or flight state." When you breathe slowly and deeply for 20 minutes and focus only on your breathing, your mind and body calm down.

Not everyone will find the time to do this, even though it would be beneficial to his health and well-being. But everyone can find the time to easily develop the habit of saying, "Right now, I am breathing. I am joyfully grateful for each and every breath."

Slow, deep breathing has a calming effect on your emotional state. When you breathe slowly and deeply you release stress and tension. If you are nervous or fearful, exhaling fully and inhaling deeply will enable you to become calmer. As you become calmer, you will be able to think more clearly about the wisest course of action for the present.

Think of something that you do many times a day. Let that remind you to think, *I am joyfully grateful for each and every breath.*

> I once asked a group of students, "If you were strongly motivated to make it a daily habit to be joyfully grateful for each and every breath, what would you do?"
> Here are some of the answers:
> - I always like to know what time it is and I frequently check my watch. So I could make it a habit to say, "I am joyfully grateful for each and every breath," after I look at my watch.
> - When I work on a computer, I tend to push the "save" button many times a session. I can release stress and feel calmer as I push the "save" button by thinking, Right now I am breathing. I am joyfully grateful for each and every breath.
> - I have a habit of clapping my hands a number of times

- *each day, so each time I clap I could say, "I am joyfully grateful for each and every breath."*
- *I don't know if I would remember on my own, so I could ask a friend to remind me throughout the day to say it together with him. I know someone who would benefit a lot from this, and the fact that I am helping him will add an incentive for me to do this.*
- *A few weeks later, one student reported that whenever he passes a door with a mezuzah, he says, "I love You, Hashem Yisbarach. And I am grateful for my breathing right now."*
- *Another student reported, "I tend to find it difficult to fall asleep. Recently I have been saying to myself, I am becoming more and more sleepy and tired with each and every breath. And each time I breathe, I am more and more grateful for my breathing and for all the other many things that I appreciate and am grateful for."*

Keep a Joy Journal

One of the most effective ways to recall your daily moments of joy is to keep a daily joy journal.

Every day, write down at least a few of your joyful moments. These can be events and situations when you experienced high levels of joy or when you felt sparks of joy. If you do not record them in your journal, these joyful moments might be easily forgotten. Since you are focusing on creating joyful moments, you will notice them and remember them because you listed them in your joy journal.

If the day is ending and you haven't written a single item in your joy journal, then go out of your way to create a moment of joy.

You can ask yourself, *If I were highly motivated to create a joyful moment right now, what could I say or do?*

You might ask yourself, *Who could I speak to right now and what could I say to bring a smile to their face?* When you cause others to be joyful, you have a great reason to feel joyful yourself.

Saying a prayer to Hashem and asking for joy for yourself or for others is something that you can add to your journal. If you ever find it difficult to add anything at all to your joy journal, say a prayer. "My Father, my King, Creator and Sustainer of the universe, please give me joyful moments so I will be able to thank You and record it in my journal."

When you have joyful courage, joyful serenity, joyful kindness, joyful *zrizus,* and joyful patience, you will have many more joyful jottings in your joy journal.

You can also suggest that others keep joy journals. This way you will have a positive influence on the live of other people. When they later thank you for the suggestion because it has added to their good feelings, you will then have another entry for that day.

> *I had a conversation with someone who told me that he frequently feels sad and frustrated.*
>
> *"Can you think of some of your life's most joyful moments?" I asked him.*
>
> *At first he was so stuck with his distressful feelings that it was hard for him to recall times he did feel happy.*
>
> *Eventually, a slight smile came to his face. "I do have a memory of feeling good." He described the situation in detail. Little by little, he got into the sounds and sights and feelings of that memory.*
>
> *"Right now, with this memory, you can begin your joy journal," I suggested to him.*
>
> *"As you keep writing down details of joyful memories, of successes, of times you felt deeply grateful, and of other positive moments, you will fill up a journal that will serve you well.*
>
> *"The main problem is that you don't easily recall the many joyful moments of your past history. Moments of joy are stored forever in your brain. Having a written collection of those events, situations, and occurrences will give you easy access to that great library of joyful moments.*
>
> *"Therefore, you should read your journal every day. The more often you read it, the more easily you will remember the good times in your life. Regardless of how long ago a positive event happened, you can bring it to the forefront of your mind in the present."*

What stops you from creating more joyful moments?

When you have a goal, it's important to know what you have to do to accomplish your goal. It's also important to know what prevents you from achieving your goal.

To clarify the answer, ask yourself, *What stops me from reaching this goal?* When you think of the answer, ask yourself, *What can I do to overcome this?*

For example, some people cannot reach meaningful goals because they lack information. They don't know the steps that they need to take to reach their goal. They should ask, "What can I do to gain the information and knowledge that I need to know?"

They can ask people who know the answers. People who have already accomplished the same goal might be the best people to ask. If you don't know who would know the answers, you can ask for referrals to people who might know.

Read books and articles on the topic you want to know more about. You can ask librarians or bookstores for suggestions.

Some reasons about not being able to reach a specific goal might be accurate. But many thoughts that prevent the reaching of a goal are just thoughts. They are just excuses. They are just rationalizations. They are just imaginary limitations.

In short, these negative thoughts are the only thing preventing some people from reaching their goal. The truth is that without the limiting thought, they would be able to do what it takes to reach their goal.

When it comes to increasing moments of joy, many people are prevented from achieving this achievable outcome only by the thought that they can't do it. In reality if they believed they could be more joyful, they would be successful.

Being joyful is not appropriate in some life situations. However, there are many distressful circumstances and situations that are over and done with, yet a person might choose to obsessively think about them in the present. He thinks that the situation prevents him from joy right now. But in actuality, if he would be totally determined to be joyful in the present, he could do it.

If I told you *not* to think about a pink elephant, a pink elephant would be the only thing on your mind. The same thing happens if you're trying *not* to think of negative thoughts. Instead of worrying about thinking thoughts you *don't* want to think, start thinking about what you *do* want to think about. Instead of thinking, *Don't think about a pink elephant – or worrying thoughts,* have in mind, *Think about a sunny day – or thoughts of joy.*

Think elevating thoughts that enable you to grow spiritually. Think thoughts of connecting with our Father, our King, Creator and Sustainer of the universe. Think about the wonders of Creation. Think about what you would like to accomplish and achieve. Think thoughts of the character traits that you want, such as kindness, compassion, courage, gratitude, serenity, joyful willpower, and other positive qualities.

Sometimes you need a friend, teacher, or mentor to help you if you keep getting stuck in negativity. Do all you can to find people who encourage and inspire you.

Be clear about what you consider your obstacles. Be determined to overcome those obstacles to joy.

The biggest obstacle is simply not focusing on increasing your joy. Right now you can choose to overcome that obstacle. Right now you can say to yourself, *I am totally determined to create more moments of joy. I will do everything that is within my power to be more joyful. I will speak and act joyfully. I will help others create more joy for themselves and I will enjoy this so much that I too will experience joy.*

> *A fellow who was frequently depressed used to feel that his long history of sadness made it much easier for him to feel down than to feel upbeat.*
>
> *A joy coach told him, "You are correct that if you have a history of sadness, it is easier for your brain to focus on sad thoughts. But the latest research on brain plasticity shows that regardless of what your brain has thought in the past, in the present you can still create a joyful way of being.*
>
> *"In the beginning this will take a lot of effort. You must be totally determined to keep thinking, speaking, and acting joyfully. Be persistent! Without persistence, you are likely to return to the old way of thinking. But you can actually change the neural pathways of your brain when you create many moments of joy.*
>
> *"Don't think about being joyful all the time. And don't focus on all the reasons why you find it difficult to be joyful. Rather, focus on what you can think, say, and do now to create more moments of joy. When you make your goal easier to reach, there is more of a chance that you will achieve your goal."*
>
> *"How long will it take for me to be successful?" the fellow asked.*
>
> *The joy coach responded, "What specifically do you consider success? Success will take as long as it takes. Regardless of how long it takes, you live one moment at a time. All you can do is create joy during the one moment at a time that you are experiencing your life."*
>
> *The fellow understood and immediately felt much lighter. "I feel better already," he said.*

A few days later he commented, "I now understand that my idea of success or lack of it has been holding me back from being more joyful. I am going to drop that mind-set. Every moment of joy is a spiritual and emotional success. I will appreciate each of these moments."

As time went on, he did experience more joy more frequently. And since he wasn't keeping score, he was able to enjoy the good moments.

Your moments of joy are unique to you

Every living person is unique, from his genetic makeup to his personal history. Since you are unique, your past and future moments of joy will be unique to you. You have your own unique style of joy in the present, too.

Some people think about the joy of other people. Then they say, "I'm just not a joyful person. I'm not as outgoing and friendly as some joyful people. I would feel strange to act like some of the joyful people I've seen." Realize that you only need to experience joy in your unique way.

Some extroverts are joyful and some are not. Some introverts are joyful and some are not. Some loud people are joyful and some quiet people are joyful.

Anyone who isn't joyful right now can choose and decide to create more joy in his own unique way.

When you think about being more joyful, you only need to contemplate your own unique style of joy.

> *Someone who was very shy spoke to me about overcoming his shyness.*
>
> *I replied, "You definitely can gain a lot by overcoming the limitations of being shy. But what is your personal motivation for wanting to be less shy?"*
>
> *"I don't really mind being shy," he said. "But I was told many times that being shy was holding me back from being happy. I feel that until I overcome my shyness, I won't be authentically happy."*
>
> *I told him, "I agree that you can gain a lot by interacting more with other people. But you can create many joyful moments in your life even before you go beyond your shyness. Joyful moments can be experienced when you are interacting with others and when you are by yourself.*
>
> *"Your joy is in your mind. You create it by the way you talk to yourself and with the mental pictures you recall and create. You have the ability to be joyful when you pray and when you study Torah. You have the ability to be joyful when you do acts of kindness for others, even when they don't realize that you have done those acts of kindness for them.*
>
> *"The more joyful you are, the easier it will be for you to overcome your shyness. Shyness comes from giving others the power to intimidate you. As you master joy from within, you will be more in charge of your own feelings. At the forefront of your mind will be the thoughts that create joy. This will free you from the thoughts that create the uncomfortable feelings of shyness.*
>
> *"Since you have associated a lack of joy with being shy, you probably have added uncomfortable feelings about your shyness. From now on, you can look at shyness and joy as two separate qualities.*
>
> *"Regardless of whether or not you become less shy, you can become more joyful. This will actually make it easier for*

you to speak and act with others in better ways."

The fellow had a big smile on his face as he saw himself being more joyful and less shy.

Have a Joyful Day!

It's nice to have a nice day. But it's great to have a joyful day.

Wish people a joyful day. Compare the standard "Have a nice day," with "Have a joyful day!" What kind of a day would you prefer to have?

It would be incongruous to say, "Have a joyful day!" in a dull tone of voice with a sad look on your face. So allow yourself to experience joy when you wish others joy.

What will happen when you regularly wish people a joyful day? Experiment and see.

Practice if you need to make a special effort to say, "Have a joyful day!"

And to you, dear reader, I wish that you "Have a joyful day!"

> Someone I didn't know recently called and complained, "I'm not very happy most of the time. What do you suggest I do?"
>
> I was pressed for time so I responded briefly. "Without

knowing your personal life history, can I make a simple suggestion that has been helpful for many people?" I asked.

"Certainly," he said. "That's why I called you."

"Make it a custom to say, 'I wish you a joyful day,' to as many people as you can. Even when you write e-mails, bless people with joy. You can make it a habit to sign off, 'I wish you much joy.'

"People who were persistent in doing this have told me how it has made a positive impact on their own life."

He called me up a week later and told me that it was amazing how well the simple technique was working for him.

Take a Joy Walk

Walking is one of the healthiest and simplest exercises. When you walk briskly, you breathe more deeply and your mind clears. Your brain produces healthy biochemicals that make you feel better and enable you to think with greater clarity. Walking stimulates creativity, and you might think of better ways to reach goals. Many people take walks to come up with solutions to challenges.

You can utilize your walking time to increase your level of joy. As you walk briskly, repeat to yourself, *With each and every step, I am feeling more and more joy. With each and every step, I am feeling more and more joy. With each and every step, I am feeling more and more joy.*

You can do the same thing with all the other positive traits and states that you would like to improve. For example, you can say to yourself, *With each and every step, I'm building my joy and my courage, my kindness and my serenity.*

Someone who spent a lot of time complaining about how bad he usually felt asked me what he could do to feel better.

I reminded him, "People who never talk about their bad feelings might gain from sharing how they feel with someone they trust. But a general rule is, 'If you're doing something and it's not working, do something else.'"

I suggested that he take joy walks instead of talk about his feelings. He did not seem open to doing something that would take a long time, so I suggested five-minute joy walks three times a day. While walking, he should repeat, "With each and every step, I am feeling more and more joy."

He started to argue. But I told him, "If you argue without experimenting, we are both wasting our time. Try it for a week. Three times a day. Then we can discuss it again."

I called him each day and, for the first few days, he came up with excuses. I finally said to him, "If you don't experiment, you are making a statement that you do want to feel bad. You claim you don't. But your non-action speaks louder than your words. Do you really want to feel better?" He claimed he did. "So prove it to me, by taking three joy walks a day. If it doesn't work, at least you got a little healthy exercise. Force yourself to do it even if it's hard. The more difficult it is for you, the greater the achievement.

"In the beginning you will need to ignore any negative self-talk about why this won't work and how silly it is. I assure you, that when you are able to keep your mind focused on the words, 'With each and every step, I am feeling more and more joy,' it will work for you."

It did.

Transform frustration into joy

Many events automatically elicit feelings of frustration. Your magnificent brain can instead automatically and spontaneously elicit feelings of joy from these situations. You can say, *"Gam zu l'tovah"* (This too is for the good). Imagine how much you will gain by transforming frustration into joy.

Just reading about this idea will not automatically cause this transformation. That's not the way brains work. Merely knowing that something is humanly possible doesn't mean that the new pattern will become internalized and integrated into your daily life.

But if you condition your brain with a new pattern, by speaking and acting in a new and better way, it will eventually become automatic.

I know a person who used to get very upset when things fell from his hands. If he dropped his pen or his keys, he would express his frustration with words that were inconsistent with being joyful.

He was willing to try new patterns, so he followed through when

I suggested a way to train his brain to react in an upbeat manner.

I told him to exclaim the words, "Yes, JOY!!!" when he dropped something. I told him to practice it 20 times while I watched.

He repeatedly dropped his pen onto the table and exclaimed as joyfully and humorously as possible, "Yes, JOY!!!"

After a minute of actual practice, he said, "That's really funny."

It worked. And he found that even when he dropped a raw egg on the floor he was able to say, "Yes, JOY!!!"

It is not always so easy. Sometimes you might have to practice for more than a minute. But it's a lot more enjoyable to experience more joy in your life than more frustration.

Find something fairly trivial that elicits a frustrated response from your brain. Begin to train your brain to respond with, "Yes, JOY!!!" Your brain will appreciate your efforts. And so will your soul.

> "I was usually a pretty calm person," someone told me. "I didn't get angry very often and if I did, I got over it fairly quickly. But I did experience a lot of frustration in my life. I had a lot to do and very little time to do it.
>
> "From the outside, a stranger couldn't tell how much stress I often experienced. But on the inside, I often felt the tension mount. This was especially true when I had to take care of things that I felt were a waste of my precious time. But in reality, I did have to do those things. Complaining to myself wasn't a bit helpful.
>
> "Finally, I decided enough is enough. I could blame the situations for my frustration and stress, but I knew the truth. I was causing myself the stress by what I was telling myself. And I was saying, 'I shouldn't have to waste my time on this.'
>
> "When I heard that one can transform frustration into joy, I made a momentous decision. I was going to master this ability.
>
> "I kept repeating the affirmation, 'Every bit of frustration I experience is created in my mind. And now my mind will choose to be joyful.'
>
> "At first I said this entire statement. But after I repeated it a number of times, I realized that I no longer needed to say

the first statement. I had totally accepted that I was creating my own frustration. So all I needed to keep repeating was, 'Now my mind will choose to be joyful.'

"The positive effects of this message were awesome. My mind kept choosing joy so frequently that it became really easy for me to be joyful. I highly recommend this practice to everyone. This will be helpful even if you only experience a small amount of frustration in your life. But if you experience high levels of stress, you need to be absolutely determined to transform frustration into joy. If I could do it, I know that everyone else could also."

"Bake joy cookies"

This is not a recipe book and I don't have a recipe to share. But if you know how to bake cookies, I suggest that you bake "joy cookies." If you don't bake cookies yourself, you can ask someone else to bake them for you.

Whatever cookie recipe you use, shape the dough into three shapes: a letter J, a letter O, and a letter Y. This, of course, spells the word "JOY."

As you prepare the cookies contemplate what it is like to experience joy.

If you eat the cookies, eat them in the proper order. First, eat the "J." Then eat the "O." And finally, eat the "Y." You can allow yourself to experience joy even if you choose to eat them in a different order. Even when you eat just one cookie, you still are permitted to think of "Joy." It's the thought that counts.

Share your "joy cookies" with others. A grandchild receiving a grandmother's "joy cookies" will have a good feeling. A grandfather who receives his granddaughter's "joy cookies" will experience an even greater feeling. I know this firsthand, and recalling the memory always brings a smile to my face.

> *"I feel bad that my friends are all going on a school trip and I can't go because of the cast on my broken foot," a young daughter told her mother.*
>
> *"I have an idea," said the mother. "Let's bake some 'joy cookies.' I'll put them in the freezer. When your foot is healed, we'll visit people in the hospital and give them 'joy cookies' with wishes for a speedy recovery."*
>
> *The daughter and mother enjoyed their time together baking the cookies and imagining the smiles on the patients' faces when they would receive the cookies that spelled J-O-Y.*
>
> *Afterward the daughter said, "I felt disappointed that I missed the trip. But the fun I had giving out the 'joy cookies' will be a memory that I will always cherish."*

Joy for eating wisely and joy for refraining from eating unwisely

Our Creator created us to need food for a constant supply of energy and nutrients. This makes us dependent on resources that are outside of ourselves. This also gives us many opportunities to be aware of the multitude of kindnesses that the Almighty is bestowing upon us. This also gives us an opportunity to experience joy with every bite of food. Eat joyfully now.

With each bite and spoonful of food, we have the ability to think, *I am now joyfully grateful for each bite and each spoonful. More and more joy with each and every bite and with each and every spoonful.*

Even if you do this occasionally throughout the day, it will increase the amount of joy that you experience that day. Those who are willing to do this at every meal will experience even more joy.

For many people, eating is not only a source of good feelings; it is also a challenge to their health and well-being. It's easy to enjoy food that is tasty but not so healthy for us, like sweet or salty foods. For some it's not only the type of food that is a challenge, but the amount. In moderation and balance, the food would be totally fine. They know that small amounts would be great. But overdoing it causes health and weight problems.

If you have a tendency to overeat, allow yourself to experience joy when you refrain from eating more than the healthy amount. You will realize tremendous gains when you joyfully refrain.

You can tell yourself, *I will feel great joy every time I say NO to the food that is better for me to avoid.*

This is having "joy in self-discipline," or "joy in self-control."

You may feel that you lack proper self-discipline and self-control. But you can still experience many moments of joy with the self-discipline and self-control that you do have now.

The goal is to experience so much fun and pleasure and enjoyment with your moments of success that your brain will tell you, "This feels so good and wonderful and terrific that I want to have this great feeling more often."

When you practice this, you won't view yourself as being deprived of good feelings. Rather, you will cherish your great feelings when you have self-discipline and self-control. When you reflect on your patterns, you will remember the fun and pleasure of eating what you should and not eating what you shouldn't.

Of course, you won't always be successful. But when you are, it's terrific and wonderful. Let your self-image be, "I am a person who is successful at times. And my goal is to experience the joy of being successful even more often."

I wish you much success and much joy.

> *An overeater told me about changing the way he viewed food:*
>
> *I had a major issue with eating. I loved to eat. I loved food that was fattening. I loved food that contained a lot of sugar but not much nutritional value. I loved salty food, but it was not healthy for my blood pressure. I tried many diets. Many*

of them worked for a while. But eventually my desire to eat won, and my diet lost. I got excited whenever I heard about another diet. I told myself that maybe, just maybe, this will be the magic diet that will work for me.

The day that I made a real change was the day someone gave me the following advice.

"Some diets worked for you because you stayed off sweet-tasting food and you limited the amounts that you ate. But eventually you gave in to your cravings for food. Transform yourself. Don't berate yourself and don't put yourself down. Food is a challenge for most people. Feeling bad about eating is obviously not the approach that will work for you.

"I suggest that you enjoy food even more than before. But choose to enjoy food that is good for you in the long term. Let food be a way that you connect with the Creator. Increase your feelings of gratitude for the Giver of food.

"Feel a sense of achievement every time you choose the food that is healthy for you. And feel a sense of achievement every time you have the self-discipline and self-control to refrain from eating what is healthier not to eat. It is difficult to forego food when you want to eat something. And surmounting the difficulty can now be a source of increased joy and an upgrade in your self-image.

"When you know that food isn't good for you, hear an inner voice telling you, 'Yes, you can have great self-discipline. Yes, you can do it. Yes, you will feel proud of yourself.' You don't need to say 'No!' to what you don't want. Say 'Yes!' to what you do really want.

"Instead of feeling bad for eating the wrong food and eating too much, feel wonderful for eating the right way. This way your inner mind will associate a healthy approach to food with joy and achievement."

This positive approach worked wonders for me. Not only was I healthier and more fit, but I also felt more joyful than ever before. Food stopped being a symbol of failure and distress. Food was now a symbol of victory and spirituality.

Bless 18 people each day to be joyful

What would your own day be like if you were to make it a daily habit to bless 18 people to be joyful? Experiment and see.

How many people do you know? How many relatives do you have? How many friends? How many people do you encounter on an average day?

You might prepare a list of 100 or more names of people to bless with joy. Or you might just bless the people whose names randomly come to mind. Or you can do both.

Mentally bless people: *I joyfully and lovingly bless you with much joy.*

Who do you know who could especially use this blessing?

Most people have personal phone books that list the people they call frequently. You can spend a minute or two going through your list and blessing those people.

If you feel that 18 is too much for you to handle right now, then choose five people a day, or 10 or perhaps 15. The main thing is to get started and begin to make this a habit.

You might make a statement at the beginning of the day, "Today, I plan to joyfully and lovingly bless the people I meet or think of." This gives a joyful message to your conscious and subconscious mind, and sets a goal for the day.

The Sages teach that one who prays for others is answered first. This would be so even if you only pray for one person. All the more so when you pray for many people. When you bless people, you are essentially praying for them.

We realize that if someone is physically ill, he needs a prayer for health. There is even a mitzvah to pray for healing. If someone lacks money, he needs our financial help and our prayers on his behalf. Someone who lacks joy has a need for joy, just as the others need health and money. Therefore, we should bless him with joy.

Before you read further, spend a few moments blessing various people who come to your mind. "I joyfully and lovingly bless [my friends and family] with much joy."

> *I was interacting with someone who needed a boost of joy. I suggested that he open a telephone directory and randomly choose names to bless with joy: "I joyfully and loving bless [the person whose name he was reading] with joy." He did it and found it an amazing experience. He came across names of complete strangers, and this gave him a mind-set that he cared about many more people than just the people he knew personally.*
>
> *"I tend to be obsessive," he told me. "When something worrisome or bothersome is on my mind, it's difficult for me to not think of these distressful thoughts. I now realize that blessing people on a long list is a highly effective antidote. Because I'm obsessive, I am more open than most people to repetitively repeat mental tasks. This new habit is just what I needed."*

Joyful Dreams

Before you go to sleep, you have a great opportunity to condition your mind to be more joyful by programming yourself to have joyful dreams. Simply repeat the words, "Joyful dreams," in a calm and peaceful tone of voice.

You might also suggest ideas for a joyful dream. With patience and persistence, you will eventually see results.

After upgrading the joy in your dreams, you can condition your mind for more courage, kindness, and serenity by suggesting to yourself, "Brain, please create more dreams of courage, kindness, and serenity."

Since serenity is a state of inner calm, it is a state that is conducive to falling asleep. So thinking about being calm and relaxed will make it easier to fall asleep. Think, *All my muscles are becoming calm and relaxed*. Repeat this in the most calm and relaxed tone possible.

What would you be like at your best and greatest? When you think about it right before falling asleep, your subconscious mind is likely to run these patterns over and over again in your dreams.

Some people try to create joyful dreams just a few times. If it doesn't work, they conclude that they're unable to condition their minds to run joyful dreams. In reality, they are giving up too soon.

Since the process of conditioning your mind for joyful dreams is so simple, it's worthwhile to persist. Just imagining having joyful dreams is a pleasurable experience. So even if you don't actually get to see a joyful dream, you still benefit from just imagining what it would be like.

> *Someone told me that he had great difficulty falling asleep. When he was active during the day, he kept his mind busy with whatever he was engaged in.*
>
> *But in the quiet of the night, he focused on what went wrong during that day. Then he would recall many things from his past that he was still resentful about and other things that he felt guilty for. When he thought about the future, many worrisome thoughts arose. He was worried about the future of our planet in general and his own future in particular. All this filled him with anxiety, and he found it difficult to fall asleep.*
>
> *He had made an effort to think more positively, but so far he wasn't successful at it.*
>
> *I recommended that he keep a gratitude journal. Before going to sleep at night, he should write down five things for which he was grateful. He did find it helpful but he still had trouble falling asleep.*
>
> *I suggested that he repeat the words, "Joyful dreams," for at least 10 minutes a night. He should meditate on this, and be as creative as he could when he thought about the most spiritually elevating joyful dreams that he could imagine.*
>
> *Dreams do not adhere totally to reality, so this would enable him to utilize more of his creative imagination. At first he argued that he didn't have a great imagination. But I told him that having a creative imagination is a skill like all other skills. The more you practice, the better you get. He could fantasize about any spiritually elevating joyful dreams that he would like to have.*

He was not conscious of any specific dreams when he woke up the next morning. But he had fallen asleep much faster than he had in a very long time. He felt that his joyful-dream affirmation was working, since he felt so much better than usual when he woke up.

Reviving downhearted spirits

One of the best ways to increase your own feelings of joy is to bring joy to those who need it the most. Hearing that you sincerely care may be enough to lift their spirits.

There are a multitude of reasons why someone might feel sad or discouraged. You might help him think of potential solutions or help out with words of encouragement.

It's awful to think that no one cares about you. When you show that you care about the welfare of someone who is feeling down, it's like giving water to a thirsty wanderer in the desert.

An emotional low can happen to almost anyone, even people who are very accomplished and emotionally strong. Even the supersuccessful have their moments of self-doubt and discouragement. Encouraging the discouraged will be a source of joy to both the encouraged one and to the kind and compassionate soul doing the encouraging.

Some people seem to have a natural knack for saying the right thing. But just like all of us, even people who are skilled at giving encouragement and hope can further develop their skill in this area.

One way to develop the skill is to keep asking different people, "What successfully gave you encouragement when you needed it?"

After interviewing at least 100 people and listening carefully to their answers, you will be more knowledgeable about what you can say and do to give more people encouragement.

If someone can't answer right away, tell him, "Please think about it. You might recall something that you found helpful by the next time we meet."

Some people feel more comfortable asking people they know well. Others find that it's easier for them to ask strangers they just met, while waiting in a line in a store or if they happen to be traveling together.

One student told me that ordinarily he would find it difficult to ask people this question. But when he was waiting for the bus near the Western Wall he found it relatively easy.

If you have an opportunity to speak to someone who is skilled at bringing joy to people, don't hesitate to ask him, "Can I ask you for some suggestions on what I could say to encourage people?"

People who realize the great kindness involved will be happy to share what they know with you. They will be partners with you in the lofty practice of reviving the spirits of those who are feeling low. Bringing a smile to others brings a smile to the one causing the smile and is a great source of spiritual joy.

> *Someone who missed a meeting of the Joy Club of Jerusalem told me that he skipped the session because he was feeling too down to attend.*
>
> *"Besides the standard things that one could do to feel better, what would you suggest I do that will help me?" he asked.*
>
> *I told him that by encouraging and inspiring other people who were feeling down, he will improve his own feelings.*

"But if I can't even help myself to feel joyful, I don't know how to help anyone else," he protested.

I told him that he could develop the hobby of asking people, "What has anyone ever said to you or to someone else in your presence that lifted your spirits?"

"Hearing ideas from 100 people will open up an entire world of possibilities for you," I told him.

"But I can't do that," he argued. "I'm not the kind of person who can ask such questions to someone else."

"The only reason you think that you're not such a person is because you've never done it yet. After you ask 10 people, the other 90 will be much easier."

"That sounds great. But I can't see myself asking even 10 people."

We took a walk so I could show him how easy it is to ask the question. We met a friendly looking fellow waiting for the light to change. I started by saying to him, "We're working on a project. Can I ask you a question?"

"Of course. Go ahead," he replied.

"What has anyone ever said to you that gave you encouragement?"

"That's a great question," he said with a smile. "The first person who comes to mind is my mother. She always told me that she believed in my abilities to accomplish whatever I was determined to accomplish. That has been a constant source of encouragement in my life."

"Now can I ask you another question? How did you feel when I asked you this question?"

"I felt my late mother's love for me. This brought up some great memories. I thank you for asking me this question. Good luck on your project."

The fellow who was walking with me commented, "That seemed easy. I thought it would be much more difficult."

I responded, "My experience has been that if you ask such questions respectfully, most people respond cheerfully. If someone keeps a stiff upper lip and has a stern look on his face, don't ask him. But if someone seems friendly, he *will appreciate this opportunity to get in touch with some of his positive memories. Besides gaining more knowledge about how to be more encouraging, asking such questions will train you to be more assertive."*

Life is now: creating moments of kindness

Rejoice for every opportunity to do an act of kindness. When you are kind to others, you are being kind to your own soul. When you do an act of kindness, you are expressing love for your Creator and love for humanity.

Some people think that they are wasting time when they do a favor that someone requested. But doing an act of kindness is one of the wisest ways to use your precious time.

Doing an act of kindness for another person might take longer than you expected. When you master the ability to feel deep pleasure for every kindness that you do, you will be free from frustration. In addition, you will actually enjoy yourself so much that few other activities would give you the same pleasure.

It might take time to build your appreciation of kindness. Be patient. You are a work in progress. An artist at work on a major masterpiece gets pleasure from each brushstroke. A builder constructing a mansion for his family will enjoy the progress of every brick he adds to his house.

When you build a mansion of kindness, you are building an eternal edifice. You are in the midst of your masterpiece. It will only be completed when you breathe your last breath.

Savor each kindness that you merit to do.

> *"I am a goal-oriented person," the fellow told me. "I have accomplished a lot, but not as much as I would have wished. This causes me constant anxiety when I waste time with other people's requests. I tend to be irritable and snappy. How can I prevent people from taking it personally that I react to their requests that way?"*
>
> *"A great question," I smilingly told him. "It's great that you are so goal oriented. But included in your many goals, the goal of loving your Creator and being kind to His children should stand at the top of the list.*
>
> *"Picture a person who is always busy, working on a project to make money. If a better opportunity to make much more money comes along, he won't view it as a disturbing element. He will feel a deep appreciation about this opportunity to make much more money."*
>
> *"I got it," the fellow responded.*

Life is now: creating moments of courage

Courage is a trait that greatly enhances a person's life. Its opposite, fear, is a key obstacle in life. Besides causing much stress and distress, fear prevents a person from achieving and accomplishing.

To say or do things that take courage, you only need a present moment of courage. You don't need to be totally fearless and you don't have to be a person who thinks of himself as being courageous. You only need a moment of courage right now!

Regardless of how you have acted in the past, you can create a moment of courage in the present. When you think about anything positive that you would like to say or do in the future, see yourself as having the courage to say or do it. The more courage you express in real life, the easier this will be. But even if a person never had a moment of courage in the past, he could still visualize a future moment of courage.

In a previous book, *Courage* (ArtScroll), I have elaborated on practical ways to build this valuable attribute. In the context of "life is now," here is a summary of that book's main ideas to enable you to create more moments of courage.

TWENTY IDEAS FOR CREATING COURAGE

1. Courage is a decision I make to go beyond fears that needlessly limit me. Every time I speak and act in a situation that is challenging for me, it builds my level of courage. I won't allow feelings of fear to stop me from saying what needs to be said and doing what needs to be done.
2. All courage is in my mind. Courage comes from the thoughts I think, and I choose my thoughts.
3. Whenever I melt unnecessary fears, in that moment I am fearless.
4. I ask my loving Father and powerful King, Creator and Sustainer of the universe, to give me the courage I need to say what is important for me to say and do what is important for me to do.
5. The memory of everything I ever said and did that took courage for me to say and do is stored in my brain. My brain is always with me. Therefore I have the ability to access courage whenever I choose.
6. Since I have already said and done things that took courage for me to say and do, I have a right to identify myself as a person who has courage.
7. This moment is the only moment that exists. To speak and act courageously, I only need to speak and act courageously this moment in the present.
8. I will become more aware of any self-talk that prevents me from speaking and acting with courage. Whenever I need courage, I will talk to myself the way people with courage talk to themselves.
9. When I need a boost of courage, I will say to myself with enthusiasm and intensity, *I have the ability to speak and act with*

courage right now. I will repeat this with more and more intensity until I actually experience it.
10. All unnecessary fear is created with my imagination. I, like everyone else, have been blessed with the ability to imagine supergreat courage. Right now I imagine having all the courage I would wish for.
11. I will learn from every person who speaks and acts with courage. I see myself talking and acting with that same courage.
12. I will remember my most courageous moments. I will double even a spark of courageous energy. Now I will double it again. I will keep on doubling these courageous feelings until I feel myself radiating courage.
13. If I find it difficult to say something, I will ask myself, *Do I have a right to say this?* If yes, I will just say it!
14. I will have the courage to bounce back from mistakes and adversity.
15. I will have the courage to do what's right even if others make fun of me. The more difficult it is, the greater I become.
16. I will have the courage to tell people respectfully to refrain from speaking negatively against others. I will feel joy for doing so.
17. I will visualize a tremendous crowd cheering for my courage. I will hear the cheers. These mental pictures and sounds will give me feelings of great courage.
18. Whenever I need a dose of added courage, I can drink an imaginary drink that gives me magnificent courage. (Real water will also work, because your imagination is always with you.)
19. I won't take needlessly foolish risks. I will differentiate between risks that are wise and those that aren't.
20. Each and every day I will do something courageous.

Someone who agreed to read this list twice a day for an entire month reported:
  "I used to look at myself as a very insecure person. I expe-

rienced many fears, which held me back in many areas of my life. I was easily intimidated by many people. I couldn't ask someone for what I wanted if I was unsure that the person would be kind and understanding. I blamed my childhood and my parents for my fears.

"When people pointed out the times that I had shown courage, I would argue, 'Yes, it did take a bit of courage for me to say or do those things, but that's not really who I am.' My identity as a wimpy type of person was a source of great distress. I limited myself tremendously.

"But all this changed after I was told that I should stop blaming anyone for my lack of courage. Rather, I should start building courage now in the present, one act of courage at a time.

"Every time it was difficult for me to say or do something positive, that was an act of building my level of courage. I didn't need to change my identity right away. I just need to take action. It helped me greatly to realize that now, in the present, my beloved Father and King, Creator and Sustainer of the universe, is bestowing me with life and is giving me the opportunity to speak and act the way I would if I would really be courageous. This made the entire project easier for me to handle.

"I agreed to read these 20 principles twice a day. Even before a month had passed I felt very differently about myself. People who knew me pointed out that they noticed a change in me. I am extremely grateful for these principles. I plan to keep reading them even after the month is up."

Life is now: creating moments of serenity

Serenity is at the root of many positive traits and patterns. When you are serene, you are free from the stress and distress of anxiety, nervousness, fear, worry, and anger. This is a state of well-being that is conducive for clear thinking.

Regardless of how stressed you have been in the past, you can create a moment of serenity in the present. Every time you are calm and serene, that moment is stored in your brain. The more moments of serenity that you have experienced in life, the easier it will be for you to access this wonderful state.

In a previous book, *Serenity* (ArtScroll), I have elaborated on practical ways to build this valuable attribute. In the context of "life is now," here is a summary of that book's main ideas to enable you to create more moments of serenity.

EIGHTEEN IDEAS FOR MASTERING SERENITY

1. Serenity is a choice that I make with my own mind. I create moments of serenity with the way I speak to myself and the mental pictures I see.

2. I am resolved to master serenity. I will benefit in multiple ways from usually being calm and serene. As I focus on those benefits, I will be more motivated to master this state.

3. This moment is the only moment that exists, and this moment I can choose to be calm and serene.

4. All stress comes from the thoughts in my mind. Therefore my thoughts can release stress right now. Whenever I realize that I feel stress, I will talk to myself in ways that enable me to become calmer.

5. I will recall times when I felt calm and serene. I will see what I saw then. I will hear what I heard then. And I will presently feel what I felt then.

6. I will mentally picture the most calm and serene scenes that I can imagine. Since these images are in my mind, I can visit these calm and serene places whenever I choose.

7. Whatever I focus on gets strengthened. I am strengthening my ability to be calm and serene by focusing on being this way.

8. As I breathe calmly and serenely, I will repeat to myself, "With each and every breath, I am becoming calmer and more serene."

9. My self-talk creates my inner state. I will talk calmly and serenely to myself and to others more and more frequently.

10. I will look at every challenging moment as a moment when I can upgrade my serenity. I will say to myself, *This too will upgrade my serenity.*

11. The nine-word serenity formula is: "Be totally in the present with a calm attitude."

12. A few seconds ago is now ancient history. I will learn from whatever happened and let it go.

13. No matter how much I have to do, I will do each thing calmly and serenely. This will enable me to take care of things

faster and more wisely. I will be alert and will do things with appropriate speed.
14. Whenever challenges with other people arise, I will allow myself to be in a centered and focused state. In this state I will think clearly about the wisest things to say and do.
15. When I drink water, I will mentally tell myself, *Every time I drink water, I will feel calmer and more relaxed.*
16. I will learn from every calm person I meet. I will learn from their attitudes and patterns of speaking. I will "wear the head" of a calm and serene person to help me think calmly.
17. I will mentally prepare myself for challenges. Whenever I think of a challenging situation, I will picture myself handling the challenge calmly and serenely. Every time I practice in my mind makes it easier to be this way in reality.
18. I will take serenity walks. As I walk, I will say to myself, *I am becoming calmer and more relaxed with each and every step.*

"My basic nature is to be nervous, worried, and full of anxiety," someone said to me. "I wish that I were a happy person, but I can't see that happening. I remember being very nervous as a child, and family members would say to me, 'You're just like your mother. She is often overwhelmed with worry. And you certainly take after her. What can you do, that's just the way you are!'

"Every once in a while I made an effort to learn ways to become calmer, but nothing seemed to work for me."

"A compassionate relative changed my life. He said to me, 'I, too, used to consider myself a natural worrier. But then I realized that no one is born a worrier. Infants tend to be in a state of well-being when they aren't hungry, tired, or otherwise uncomfortable. When we get older, some of us build up the pattern of focusing on what could go wrong. These thoughts create anxiety. But we don't have to remain that way.

"'With consistent practice, we can learn ways of thinking that enable us to remain calm. People who have a habit of worrying need to practice more than others who tend to be *calm and serene. But serene thinking is a learnable skill. I have gained greater mastery over the ability to focus on what I can think, say, and do in the present to be calm. I know that you will be able to master this skill just as I have.'*

"It was a real pleasure to find someone who reassured me that I could succeed in becoming a calm and serene person. If an always-calm person had told me that I could do it, I wouldn't have believed him. But this relative had had to put in the effort, just like me. He was persistent and succeeded. I was totally determined to succeed also.

"I made up my mind that no matter how long it would take me, I would keep reviewing the ideas that are conducive for serenity. After a relatively short while, I saw progress. I know that others who do the same will also succeed in becoming calmer and more serene. I consider this a major achievement in my life."

When you think of your past, think: "joy!"

You have had many positive experiences in your life. Experiences when you were successful, learned positive lessons, and felt happy and joyful. Most likely, you have also had many experiences that weren't as joyful.

If someone were to tell you, "Think of your past," you have a choice. You can select joyful memories, or the opposite. People who are skilled at experiencing joy in the present consciously choose to remember their moments of joy when they think of the past.

Regardless of how you have looked at the past until now, right this moment you can decide to allow your past moments of joy to be at the forefront of your mind. When you think of your life history, allow the joyful highlights to shine bright. See the pictures and scenes of your joyful highlights right now as very big, very bright, and really close. Hear now what you heard during your joyful highlights, loudly and clearly.

Together with these pictures and sounds, allow yourself to feel the joyful feelings that you originally felt. Spin these joyful feelings from head to toe and let them keep flowing.

The larger the images and the louder the sounds you remember in your highlights, the greater your present experience of joy. You might even feel better now than you originally felt.

No matter how few or how many joyful moments a person has experienced, he can replay the best and most joyful moments many times. Right now it's not the number of joyful moments that make a difference. Rather, it is the habitual recalling of joyful moments that gives you good feelings in the present.

For example, one person might have had 9,858,292 joyful moments so far. Another person might have had only 8,259 joyful moments. Both people have the same ability to habitually recall the greatest moments over and over again. Each one can upgrade the joy he presently feels for all the many things he is grateful for now.

In the present it's not the amount of joyful moments of the past that counts. Rather it's the quality of your present thinking that creates your present emotional experiences.

The more frequently you recall your past joyful moments, the more easily your brain's neural pathways to joy can be traveled, allowing you to revisit those joyful moments.

The knowledge that repeating a memory has actual effects on your brain can motivate you to return to your favorite memories.

Condition your mind to think of your most joyful memories whenever you think about the past. What are the most joyful memories of your life until now? Write down a list of the highlights of your personal life history.

People enjoy looking at pictures of happy occasions to remember the good times they had. But even without a photograph of your most joyful memories, the memories are stored in your brain. You have the ability to access them at will.

Say to yourself, *Whenever I think of my past, it will be easy for me to recall my most joyful moments!*

Repeat this affirmation a number of times each day: *Whenever I think of my past, it will be easy for me to recall my most joyful moments.*

The more you practice, the easier it gets.

Someone shared with me that he went to a very insightful counselor. This expert showed him how he was really unhappier than he realized.

"I'm much less happy now than I used to be," he told me. "But at least I'm more authentic. I'm very real. I don't fool myself by living superficially and thinking that I was happier than I used to think I was."

"How have you gained from this approach?" I asked him.

"Looking objectively at how my life is unfolding, I can't honestly say that I've gained in practical ways. I do feel better about myself, because I am more authentic than a lot of people I know."

"How much time do you presently spend on being grateful for all the good in your life?"

"I don't have enough time and energy to spend feeling grateful. I am busy being real about my feelings of misery."

"What is this doing for your relationships with family and friends?"

"I'm afraid that living a more truthful existence, of really getting in touch with my misery, is hurting my interactions with others. But my counselor thinks that I am progressing in my quest for authenticity. He reinforces my focus on what is wrong and has been wrong in the past."

"Can I make a suggestion? For an entire week, place your attention on gratitude. And then each day think for a few minutes about how grateful you were the day before. The next day, you have more past moments of gratitude to be grateful for. And the next day even more. Take a vacation from getting in touch with your misery."

He agreed to try it out. Now that he was thinking about gratitude, he found his level of happiness increased.

At the end of a week, he felt that his entire focus about his past had improved. Not only did he feel joyful about this past week, but this experiment made him remember many more grateful and joyful moments of the past.

Then I suggested that he spend the next week focusing on past moments of joy, courage, kindness, and serenity.

He joyfully reported, "I find that my spirituality and my emotions are so much better when I select the joyful highlights of my life. This has been especially beneficial in how I've been getting along with my family."

Obsessing about what might go wrong in the future

It's wise to think constructively about the future so that you are ready to handle it intelligently. This is called planning.

Occasionally thinking worrisome thoughts is totally normal. Spending a lot of time experiencing anxiety about something that didn't happen and might never happen is a problem.

Constantly thinking about what might go wrong in the future is not healthy. It could become a pattern of obsessing. This is when you just worry: about what might go wrong, what might be missing, what might be disappointing, and what might be a source of unhappiness.

When you focus on a negative possibility happening in the future, right now in the present your brain and body react as if it is actually happening or about to happen. This distress causes the entire body to prepare for fight or flight, which is a necessity when there is real present danger. But it is counterproductive and unhealthy if it happens frequently and needlessly.

People who frequently obsess about the future can easily think that it's their nature to be this way. But it's not their born nature. No infant worries. It takes more intellectual maturity to worry.

Worry is just a learned pattern. We might have picked it up from a fellow worrier in our family. We might have picked it up from friends. Or we might have developed it all on our own. Regardless of how we developed the pattern of worrying, we can now gain greater mastery of our thoughts.

Ultimately, the basis of all worry is the fear that we will be unhappy. It's not even the events or situations that we really worry about. It is ironic that our strong desire to be happy is at the root of the thoughts that create unhappiness.

Gain greater clarity that it is fear of unhappiness that you worry about. Then you will find it easier to decide to choose joy, gratitude, serenity, and kindness now.

Besides, even if something does go wrong, you might be able to cope even better than you had imagined. Moreover, when something challenging actually happens, it is often a blessing in disguise. It can be an opportunity to develop your character in a way that you wouldn't have developed otherwise.

Develop the habit of spending most of the time thinking wisely. Think wisely about the present, the past, and the future.

If you tend to worry about the future, keep bringing your mind back to the present moment. Right now you can only deal with what is under control right now. You might be able to do some things in the present to prevent problems from developing later on. But if there is nothing practical you can do, then use your mind wisely to make the wisest use of your present moments.

> *Someone who used to be a worrier told me, "I suffered so much distress in my life because I worried about things that didn't happen. I realized that I was causing this distress with my own thoughts, but I felt I wasn't able to stop it.*
>
> *"I was advised to study the classic mussar work Chovos Halevovos (Duties of the Hearts), specifically the section*

dealing with bitachon, trust in Hashem. This was very helpful and I found it much easier to overcome the distress of worry. But my mind still focused a lot on what could possibly go wrong. I realized more than ever before that all that happened to me was ultimately for my good and I was able to cope much better than previously.

"But what helped me tremendously was a suggestion by a friend. He told me that he always imagined that things would work out exceptionally well. He would feel great about the possibility of all the good things that he would experience.

"'But don't you suffer from disappointment when things don't work out the great way you created in your mental fantasy?' I asked him.

"'Usually not,' he told me. 'I know that imagining great things doesn't mean that it will actually happen that way. But since I feel so good just keeping this in my imagination, I don't suffer from disappointment. I enjoy the good feelings that my imagination gives me. This is the opposite pattern that worriers use. Worriers feel bad in the present because of something negative they imagine. Even though most worries don't become reality, they still worry. I think that it's stupid to needlessly cause yourself pain. I think that it's smart to be in control of giving yourself positive feelings. I don't take any foolish or risky actions based on my imagination. So I find there is no downside to it. I don't waste a lot of time imagining good things. It's just a few seconds of time. The good feelings I get give me the energy to actually accomplish great things. It works better for me than coffee. People waste a lot of time on distress-causing imaginings. I spend a fraction of that amount of time creating good feelings.'

"This made sense to me. I started following his example. It made me laugh to realize that the same pattern that used to cause me so much suffering was now the source of a highly enhanced emotional life."

How can I be certain that I will never think another negative thought?

I have been asked a number of times, "How can I be certain that I will never think another negative thought?"

This is an easy question to answer. It is impossible to never think another negative thought. Therefore the simple answer is: You can't be certain that you won't think another negative thought. And if you insist on certainty, you can be certain that your brain will come up with many negative thoughts. Not just once or twice, but many times.

"Does that mean that I am doomed to not be happy?" some people then ask.

No, it doesn't mean that you are doomed. Since some people are consistently happy, it must prove that you don't have to let your negative thoughts rob you of your birthright to be happy.

The problem isn't thinking negative thoughts. The problem comes from continuing to focus on negative thoughts. Our mind has an entire stream of thoughts. Savor the positive, the joyful, the meaningful, the spiritual thoughts, and let go of those that are the opposite.

Be humble. Accept that you are a normal human being and not a superhuman or an angel (a Heavenly angel; you *can* be a kind and warm person who others might call an angel). Accept that you are fallible. Accept that you make mistakes. Accept that you aren't perfect.

Will this acceptance cause you to make more mistakes? No, it won't. It will just enable you to let go of superhigh, unreachable standards. Perfectionism leads to anxiety. It doesn't lead to being perfect and it's not the pathway to joy.

Joyful people do think counterproductive thoughts sometimes. They do think thoughts that are incompatible with joy. But they don't get stuck on those thoughts. They move on to higher, more joyful thoughts. They move on to elevated and spiritual thoughts.

Be joyful when you realize you can redirect your thoughts. In the present, you can choose joyful and elevating thoughts, words, and actions. Be joyful about that.

> *Someone who frequently felt miserable about being so imperfect with his thinking, told me, "That is such a relief to hear those calming thoughts. I always strived for high levels. I didn't realize that what I was striving for was an impossible goal. I thought that many other people were perfect, and that I was such a failure for not always thinking the highest and most elevated thoughts. You have helped me have a more realistic and balanced view of what I can reasonably expect of myself.*
>
> *"My teachers painted a beautiful picture when describing what an elevated person would be like. I honestly tried with all my might to live up to their high standards. But instead of being a joyful, spiritual being, I was full of anxiety and worry. I felt worthless and lowly. I really tried my hardest,*

I honestly did. But no matter how hard I tried I was still far from perfect."

I told the fellow, "From now on, instead of feeling so bad that you aren't perfect, allow yourself to experience joy for every positive thought, word, and action. The good feelings they bring will motivate you to keep striving for even more positive thoughts, words, and action."

And that is exactly what happened.

The "4 for self-creation" program

I have developed a personal development program that is called "4 for Self-Creation." The number 4 stands for two groups of four.

There are four major factors that create your life: your self-talk, your self-image, your goals, and your traits and states.

1. YOUR SELF-TALK

This is your constant flow of thoughts. Realizing that you have the ability to choose what you are saying to yourself in the present enables you to upgrade the quality of your entire life, moment by moment.

Being aware of your present patterns of self-talk is the first step in upgrading what you habitually say to yourself.

The second step is to be totally and intensely resolved to improve the quality of your self-talk.

For example, say to yourself, *I would love to upgrade my self-talk.* Now say something else, like, *Yes, that would be great. I will make the effort to upgrade my flow of self-talk. And I feel good that I am talking to myself about creating my way of being in the direction that I wish to go.*

If you instead said something pessimistic about your upgrading your self-talk, you can now say to yourself, *I'm glad that I realized what I said to myself. I will keep conditioning my mind to speak more positively to myself. As I keep practicing positive self-talk, it will become an automatic positive habit.*

2. YOUR SELF-IMAGE

How you view yourself is a key factor in what you will be thinking, feeling, saying, and doing. Every positive statement you make and every positive action you take is part of the lifetime process of building who you are.

We each have a belief about who we are and what we are able to do and accomplish. Regardless of what we thought a moment ago, right now in the present we can upgrade our belief about ourselves. Become more aware of your strengths and positive qualities. Identify with them. Keep on developing your skills and talents, your positive traits and states.

The Torah concept of who we are is that we are created in the Creator's image. We are children of the Creator. Each and every individual needs to realize that the universe was created for him. This means that the world is ours to appreciate and benefit from. This also means that we are responsible for the entire world. We need to do whatever we can do for as many people as we can. An essential thing that we can all do is pray to the Almighty for the welfare of others.

When we were young, the most important people in our lives were very instrumental in creating our self-image. Now in the present you have the ability to improve how you view yourself.

Make it a habit to say to yourself, *My self-image keeps growing and developing each and every day with every positive thing that I say and do.*

3. YOUR GOALS

A young child has the goals of a young child. A teenager has the goals of a teenager, regardless of how lofty. An adult has the goals of whatever he believes is possible and important. The more we build our inner resources, the more we will be able to achieve and accomplish. Meaningful goals create a meaningful life.

Every goal that you reach increases your belief in your ability to keep making and reaching more goals. Therefore, setting and reaching even minor goals fosters your habit of making and reaching goals. Some of the greatest achievers in the world began by practicing with tiny goals.

Build your skill by marking off 10 or 20 or even 50 goals a day for a week.

For example, say, "Now I make it my goal to make a blessing on drinking water and then I will drink a glass of water." As soon as you make a blessing on the water and drink the water, you have reached two goals.

"Now I make it my goal to put on my right shoe and then my left shoe." You can consider putting on your shoes one goal or two goals. Either way, you have added to your mental collection of reaching goals.

Then there are breakthrough goals. These are the really big goals that will have a major positive impact on your life. Mentally picture yourself reaching a breakthrough goal. Then follow through. Every breakthrough goal upgrades your self-image. When you view yourself as a person who can make and reach important goals, you upgrade your entire life.

4. YOUR TRAITS AND STATES

Your character traits are your personal patterns of thoughts, feelings, words, and actions. Developing positive traits is an essential part of our mission in this world. A person who usually experiences happiness and joy is said to be a happy and joyful person. His thoughts, feelings, words, and actions all reflect his trait of happiness and joy.

Even if you haven't made a specific positive *trait* habitual, you can still access or create that positive *state* in any given moment.

Your mental and emotional states are temporary feelings and behaviors; they are your moment-by-moment experiences of an event. When we are in our best states we think, speak, and act at our best. Even a person who is not usually happy and joyful can still have moments of happiness and joy. When he experiences joy, he is in a joyful state.

Mastering the ability to be in the mind-body state that is best and most appropriate for any given moment is one of the most valuable skills that a person can master.

It is impossible to always be in the state we would wish to be in. But little by little we can increase our ability. This book focuses on creating more moments of four of the most important traits/states:

1. JOY

When we think, speak, and act in ways that are conducive for joy, we will feel more joyful.

Right now in any present moment, you can choose to create a moment of joy. This book tells you how.

2. COURAGE

When we think, speak, and act in ways that are consistent with courage, we build this quality in our mind and brains. This makes it easier for us to access this state at will.

When you experience a moment of courage, in that moment you can speak and act in ways that bring out your best traits. In your moments of courage, you are not stopped by thoughts or feelings of fear.

Courage to strive for your most meaningful goals elevates your quality of life. Every time you speak or act courageously, you are building your trait of courage.

3. LOVE

Love for our Creator is a constant mitzvah. Every time you say, "I love You, Hashem *Yisbarach*," you fulfill this commandment.

When you are grateful to the Creator for your very life and for all that you have: a brain, hands, feet, eyes, ears, and anything specific that you benefit from, you will experience positive feelings. Love for our Creator is the highest spiritual level a person can attain in this world. The more we reflect on this lofty concept, the more we elevate the quality of our lives.

When a person loves the Creator, he will love speaking and acting with kindness. This was the attribute of Abraham. He had kindness and compassion for everyone he encountered.

Creating more moments of love for the Creator and love for kindness is healthy for your soul and your body.

4. SERENITY

Serenity is an inner calm that is conducive for clear thinking. This is a state of well-being. We were frequently in this state when we were infants and were free from distress. Once we developed the ability to think, we can think our way to serenity – or the opposite. It's not realistic to strive to always be serene, each moment of each day. But we can create many moments of serenity.

There are many types of serenity. There is a calm and relaxed serenity that is conducive for releasing stress and tension. There is serene empowerment that enables us to be in a state that I refer to as Centered, Focused, and Flowing. In this state we can be at our wisest and best when we interact with others. In a state of serene *zrizus*, we take action without wasting time or procrastinating. When studying and praying, a calm mind and relaxed body enables us to focus on what we are engaged in. This is a serene state that is healthy for body and soul.

Self-development is a lifetime project. But just as we live our entire lives one moment at a time, we develop the areas that will make the biggest difference in our lives one thought, word, or action at a time.

Rabbi Akiva observed that the water dripping on a rock made a hole in the rock because it was a persistent dripping. Each drop made a very slight and tiny difference. Eventually it made a very noticeable difference.

So, too, your persistent thoughts and actions will make a major difference in your life. Each thought of joy, courage, serenity, and love for Hashem and kindness will be just one thought. But over time, you will think many thoughts and do many actions that add up to create a person with positive character traits.

> I am frequently asked about books for further reading about these topics. The present book, Life Is Now: Creating Moments of Joy, Courage, Kindness, and Serenity, has new material not found in my other books. But it also gives a summary of key ideas for happiness and joy, courage and serenity.
>
> My book Conversations with Yourself elaborates on the entire subject of self-talk.
>
> Some people mistakenly think that self-talk only refers to making positive affirmations. But self-talk refers to all the many thousands of thoughts that we think each day. Realize that we don't have to control many thousands of thoughts. We only need to choose and select one thought at a time. And that one thought is always in the present.
>
> My book Building Your Self-Image and the Self-Image of Others elaborates on our immense value and worth as a gift from our Creator. Building our self-image is a lifetime process of improving ourselves with all the positive things we learn and do in life.
>
> My book Taking Action elaborates on how we can strive for many worthwhile goals and take action on our ideals to improve our way of being.
>
> I also recommend my previous books that deal with various traits that will build your character: My Father, My King: Connecting with the Creator; Happiness; Kindness; Courage; Patience; Serenity; Enthusiasm; Harmony with Others; and Thank You: Gratitude.
>
> Reading a book just one time gives you an overview of a topic. But anything that you seriously want to integrate and internalize needs repetition. Every time you read a book, you know more than the last time you read it. This will deepen your understanding.

The four-finger button technique for joy, courage, love, and serenity

The Creator gave you a portable machine that enables you to consistently access your greatest states just by pushing the right buttons. Now you just need to program the handy machine, found on your left hand.

Right now, designate your left thumb as the "button pusher." The access "buttons" are your other four left fingertips.

The tip of your index finger is the button that gets your brain to think about joy. As your thumb pushes this button, recall some of your favorite memories of being joyful. Mentally visualize what it was like when you were joyful. Hear what you heard when you were especially joyful. Feel what it felt like to be especially joyful.

From now on, whenever you are especially joyful, press your left thumb on that finger. Each time you do this when you are joyful, your "joy button" becomes more powerful.

When you want a moment of joy, press your left thumb on the first finger and allow yourself to be joyful. Even a slightly joyful feeling is a feeling of joy. Be patient. It might take a number of real-life joyful experiences for this to become automatic.

Now, designate the second finger as the finger that accesses thoughts and feelings of courage. When you want a moment of courage, press your left thumb on your courage finger. Recall times when you spoke and acted with courage. Think of your favorite courageous role models. Press your middle finger as you say the word "courage" and allow your courage to transcend fears. Each moment of courage will be added to your mental library of courage.

Now, designate the third finger as the finger that will remind you to say, "I love You, Hashem *Yisbarach,* my Father, my King, Creator and Sustainer of the universe." When you want to think of love for Hashem and loving kindness, press your left thumb on your third finger. This will also remind you to speak and act with kindness and compassion to everyone you speak to and interact with. ("I love You, Hashem, and I love kindness.")

Pushing on your fourth fingertip will remind you to access feelings of inner calm and serenity. From now on, when you want a moment of inner calm and clear thinking, press your left thumb on your little finger. Remember times and moments when you felt an inner peace. Think of the most calming and relaxing scenes from any moment in your life. Every time your left thumb touches the tip of your left pinkie, this will remind you to think calmly and serenely. You can say to yourself, *Right now, I am allowing myself to become calmer and more clear thinking.*

For some people this will be sufficient. But to really upgrade your life, I recommend that you also make four more virtual finger buttons on your right hand.

Now, let your right thumb touch the finger next to it while you say, "Self-talk." As you do this, it's worthwhile to say to yourself, *Now, I am upgrading my patterns of self-talk.*

Let your right thumb touch the tip of the middle finger and say,

Self-image. To create a positive habit, add, *Now, I am upgrading my self-image. Each and every day I see myself in a more positive way.*

Let your right thumb touch the tip of the third finger and say, *Goals.* When you think of your goals, think of something positive you can do to go forward on the goal of your choice. And say to yourself, *I am enjoying the entire process of going for my high-priority goals.*

Let your right thumb touch the tip of your little finger and say, *Traits and states,* as you think of a positive state you would like to be in right now. Realize that any state you've ever experienced is stored in your magnificent brain, which you can always access. Moreover, you can always create new states.

Besides the four positive states of joy, courage, love, and serenity, a few all-purpose states are:

1. Centered, focused, and flowing state.
2. High-impact presentation state.
3. My best and wisest state.
4. Serenely patient state.
5. Serenely empowered state.
6. Thinking clearly and creatively state.
7. Peak performance state.

The four-finger button technique is an easy tool to use. It takes just a few moments. And with the power of repetition, it's extremely effective.

> *I was having a coaching meeting with a few clients who used to have heated discussions when planning an important project. This led to lengthy arguments and hurt feelings. These clients wanted to discuss their project goals with clearer thoughts and better feelings.*
>
> *Therefore, I taught them the four-finger button technique for accessing joy, courage, love for Hashem and for each other, and serenity.*
>
> *Every time they started to become emotionally tense during the meeting, we took a five-second break and repeated together, "Joy, courage, love for Hashem and people, and serenity." They pressed their thumbs at the tips of the desig-*

nated finger as they repeated the sentence.

The meeting was one of the most successful meetings that we ever had together. And they knew that they had a highly effective tool that they could use every day of their lives.

The joy, courage, love, and serenity chant

How many times a day do you repeat the words: "Joy, Courage, Love, and Serenity"? The more frequently you repeat these words, the greater amount of time your mind will be focused on four of the qualities that will make the biggest difference in your life.

You will gain the most from chanting these words if you say them slowly with the intent to internalize these qualities.

Imagine what it would mean to you specifically if you were to experience joy, courage, love for Hashem and for doing acts of kindness, and serenity. Saying the words associated with those feelings and experiences will put those memories at the forefront of your consciousness.

Keeping joy, courage, love, and serenity at the forefront of your consciousness will have a great impact on you. Remembering these qualities will influence the way you think, feel, speak, and act.

What will your life be like if you made it a daily habit to repeat "Joy, Courage, Love, and Serenity" five times for one minute each session? You will only be able to find out by experimenting. Please note that this will only be an investment of five minutes a day. Spend five minutes a day programming and conditioning your mind to integrate and internalize four of the greatest qualities available. Be ready to notice the positive progress you will experience in your life.

People who sincerely wanted to improve reminded themselves to chant this list whenever they walked through a doorway. Every time they opened a door and walked through, they said to themselves, *Joy, Courage, Love* ('*I love you, Hashem, and I love kindness*'), *and Serenity.*"

Doing this mindfully for an entire month will make a big difference in anyone's life. If you are going to follow just one suggestion in this book, I would suggest that you create this positive habit.

> *I suggested that someone repeat the words of this section a number of times each day. I also told him that he could make believe that he was a master of these four qualities. Just as young children are easily able to play pretend games, we adults can really do so also.*
>
> *He suddenly exclaimed, "I finally got it. I finally understand why I have always had a difficult time just acting the way I would if I had a positive pattern.*
>
> *"It's because I kept telling myself that it's not authentic. I'm not really the way I want to be. I am really the way I am. It's not what I am proud of. But I'm stuck with it.*
>
> *"Young children who are playing games and acting like storekeepers, teachers, parents, or playing any other make-believe games, don't do this as a serious exercise. They are pretending. They view what they are doing as having fun. That enables them to be open to try out adultlike behavior. I now realize that I have been needlessly limiting myself.*
>
> *"All I have to do is just pretend that I am a little kid playing a game. I will play make-believe joy, make-believe courage,*

make-believe love for Hashem and love for other people, and make-believe serenity. I can't wait."

His playing make-believe did wonders for him. Especially when it came to courage, he reported, *"I've really spoken and acted with a level of courage that I would never have imagined I would be able to do. I am totally committed to continue acting this way.*

"Now I have a daily habit of telling myself, 'I am a genius at joy, courage, love for Hashem, kindness, and serenity.' It's having a powerful impact on my life. I still don't look at myself as being a genius in these areas. But I have seen tremendous improvement so far. I truly believe that if I keep repeating this and speaking and acting in ways that are consistent with these wonderful traits, this will become my actual reality. I visualize how much I will keep on gaining and this keeps me motivated to persistently think, speak, and act in better ways than ever before."

The life-transforming personal program

The life-transforming personal program that you are about to read is highly effective for conditioning your mind to improve your entire way of being. Repeat the three-step program at least five times a day for best results.

Step 1: Say this phrase slowly so you savor each word: "Right now, with Hashem's help, I create a moment of Joy, Courage, Love ("I love you, Hashem, and I love kindness!"), and Serenity, as I improve my self-talk and self-image, and have fun making progress on my high-priority goals. I now see myself being the way I wish to be."

Step 2: Be aware of your self-talk when you say this. If your self-talk is in alignment with the message of the personal program, that's wonderful.

If at first your self-talk exhibits disbelief in your ability to internalize and integrate this message, be grateful for the awareness of your present self-talk. Be patient. As you repeat this phrase five times a day for a month, you will notice progress. Every little bit of progress adds up.

Step 3: Write this phrase on a card and read it again during challenging moments. Every time you read this, you are conditioning your mind. What might seem unfamiliar at first will become very familiar with frequent repetition.

Right now, see yourself mastering the message of this personal program. Talk to yourself the way you will talk when you master this personal program. Feel the way you will feel when you master this personal program.

Imagine yourself five years from now after you have mastered the message of this personal program. Imagine looking back at the way you mastered joy, courage, love for Hashem, love for kindness, and serenity. See how you will look, sound, and feel when you have reached your high-priority goals for the "past" five years. What will your self-talk be like? What will your self-image be?

Since today is the first day of your next five-year journey, what will you do today to get off to a great start?

Have a wonderful time with the entire process!

> *A student said to me, "Whenever someone suggests that I repeat statements to myself, I tend to feel bad. I keep telling myself, 'This is ridiculous. This won't work. I'm too smart to fool myself.' After trying a few times, I give up and stop. Why should I keep trying a technique that makes me feel worse?"*
>
> *I replied, "I don't recommend that you repeat things that make you feel worse. Instead, I suggest that you practice repeating this life-transforming personal program a bunch of times in a room all by yourself. With all the intensity that you can, say this personal program as loudly as you want. Give yourself a full 10-minute tryout, three times a day. I know that 30 minutes a day for the first few days is a long time. But you are suffering most of the day with your coun-*

terproductive self-talk. You are limiting yourself greatly in all areas.

"If you knew for sure that eventually this will work for you, would you consider it worthwhile to invest the time?"

"Certainly," the fellow said with a grin.

"As soon as you overcome the emotions holding you back, you are guaranteed to see progress. The main thing is to have the attitude, 'This will certainly work for me as I keep practicing.'

"People who want to master creative writing, computer programming, piano or guitar playing, golf or tennis games, or even simple electronic games spend a tremendous amount of time practicing. Conditioning your mind for enhancing your life is worth a lot more. Wouldn't you agree?"

He did agree. He agreed to have fun practicing and spent enough time practicing this personal program. He saw great results. You will too … when you practice.

See, hear, and feel "joy, courage, kindness, and serenity" in the past, present, and future

It would be wonderful to see, hear, and feel the wonderful traits and states of joy, courage, kindness, and serenity whenever you think of the past, present, and future.

To make it easier to create these wonderful ways of being, give yourself these instructions:

"I see, hear, and feel myself becoming more and more joyful in the past, present, and future."

"I see, hear, and feel myself becoming more and more courageous in the past, present, and future."

"I see, hear, and feel myself becoming more and more kind in the past, present, and future."

"I see, hear, and feel myself becoming more and more serene in the past, present, and future."

Repeat these four specially designed programs to condition your mind in all three time periods in the major visual, auditory, and kinesthetic modalities. Even though the past is already over, you presently can condition your mind to think of joy, courage, kindness, and serenity whenever you think of the past. Even though the future hasn't happened yet, you can presently condition your mind to think of joy, courage, kindness, and serenity whenever you think of the future.

These mental conditioners will have an amazingly powerful effect on your entire way of being. The only requirement is that you repeat these conditioners in a joyful or serene state of mind. Even if you are not in a joyful or serene state when you first begin your conditioning program, with a number of repetitions that sound joyful, you will presently create a more positive state. This exercise will store these thoughts in your brain and make it much easier for your mind to access them again and again from now on.

Reinforcement is necessary for this to become an integral part of your behavior. And this reinforcement depends upon what you think, say, and do in the present.

> *I have noticed that individuals who experienced childhood traumas had very different life histories as they grew up. Some people viewed themselves as victims. They felt that they would suffer later on because of their earlier childhood experiences. This view played out in reality: They kept noticing their suffering and disappointments. Whenever they went anyplace, they would point out what went wrong and what didn't work out. They would blame all the suffering in their lives on the traumas they suffered in the past. This focus on how unfortunate they were became strengthened with every minor and not-so-minor distressful situation. They proved over and over again how their unhappiness was all because of their victimized childhood.*
>
> *But other people who had similar past traumas had the*

attitude that they were blessed. Even though they faced adverse situations, they realized that they still had much for which to be grateful. Their suffering was seen as life events that enabled them to be more spiritual and deeper than if they wouldn't have had those experiences. They became kinder and more compassionate exactly because they knew what it was like to have suffered. They had an attitude that the past is over and while our past has an impact on our lives, what we think, say, and do right now in the present is the key to our identity.

They took responsibility for creating their own lives right now in the present. Having known suffering in the past made it even more important for them to be joyful now. They viewed themselves as role models who could teach people that the suffering of the past does not prevent you from having joy in the present.

When I shared the affirmations of this section with some individuals with a victim mentality, they would claim, "This won't work for me. I am a victim and a superficial exercise is not for me." Their unwillingness to repeat these affirmations prevented them from improving their view of the past, present, and future. People with victim mentalities will be able to quote experts who will agree with their right to retain their victim status for a long, long time.

But those who were open to the attitude of, "Right now my thoughts are up to me and right now I can upgrade my past, present, and future," found that sufficient repetitions eventually had a major impact.

Experts on the plasticity of the brain are proponents of anyone's ability to condition and program his mind regardless of his past. But those individuals who repeated the positive, effective affirmations in the present did not need experts to prove that this could be done. They themselves knew with 100 percent clarity that this could be done, because they themselves experienced the ability to do this.

So my message to anyone who had a rough past and to anyone who can influence people with rough pasts, is, "It certainly takes more work to create a more positive mind-set for those who have had early rough experiences. But with sufficient repetitions everyone can create a more positive mind-set conducive to a greater amount of joy, courage, love, and serenity."

Keep in mind: To prove that something is impossible to do, you need to have 100 percent of those who tried to do it failing to do it. On the other hand, to prove that something is possible, you only need one person to be successful to prove that it's possible. The lives of many people have already proven that the past does not prevent us from having a positive present and future when we believe that we create our past and future in the present.

Upgrading your identity and learning from others

Right now you can upgrade your identity as a joyful, courageous, kind, and serene person.

When you upgrade your identity, you don't just experience these positive qualities right now. Whatever you identify with has an impact on how you spontaneously think, feel, speak, and act. So make a commitment to upgrade your identity.

Repeat this identity-creating affirmation: "Right now I see myself as being a person who is joyful, courageous, kind, and serene. This is how I am and how I wish to be. Even though I won't always be in these states, the times that I am will strengthen my identity as being joyful, courageous, kind, and serene."

If you have experienced these states even once in your entire lifetime, you have a right to say to yourself, *This is me. This is who I am.*

We all experience really good moods and moods that aren't so good. Our moods and states change, but our positive sense of self never has to be diminished. Even the most joyful, courageous, kindest or serene individuals are sometimes not in the mood to feel that way. But they still have a right to consider themselves joyful, courageous, kind, and serene.

A person can honestly say, "I am usually a joyful person, but right now I'm not in a joyful state."

A person can honestly say, "I am usually a courageous person, but right now I'm not in a courageous state."

A person can honestly say, "I am usually a kind person, but right now I'm not in a kind state."

A person can honestly say, "I am usually a serene person, but right now I'm not in a serene state."

This way we can acknowledge rather than deny our less-than-ideal thoughts, feelings, words, and actions. Our ideals remain the same.

Even great people have ups and downs. They have moments of being inspired and elevated, and they have moments when they are exhausted, tired, hungry, even overwhelmed. But they bounce back. Having a self-image of being essentially joyful, courageous, kind, and serene enables someone with this self-image to bounce back faster.

Along with identifying yourself as someone who is joyful, courageous, kind, and serene, keep learning from others. Every joyful, courageous, kind, and serene person you ever meet, read about, or hear about can be your role model. Even if you are usually more joyful, courageous, kind, and serene than someone else, you still can learn something from him that will be useful at some time.

Habitually say to yourself, "I keep learning from every person who speaks and acts joyfully, courageously, kindly, and serenely to add to my own joy, courage, kindness, and serenity."

> *A student who attended a "4 for Self-Creation" class gave me this feedback.*
>
> *"When I first heard about creating moments of joy, courage, love, kindness, and serenity, I felt very inspired and*

motivated. I felt like I was flying. Then a few days later I landed. I felt much more like I usually felt, which was the opposite of these qualities. Since I had experienced better feelings, I now felt totally disappointed and discouraged. I saw that even if I improved for a short while, it wouldn't last.

"Then I remembered that you said, 'Being aware of your thoughts and how each thought affects your feelings won't guarantee that you always think thoughts that create happiness. Rather, this awareness will enable you to have constant feedback. You will be more aware of the feelings caused by your thoughts.'

"I used to consider myself to be a person who was very negative. I just accepted that was who I was. I knew that if I worked on upgrading my thoughts, I would be a little better off. But I still viewed myself as someone who was negative.

"You mentioned that we need to keep building our identities. We all start off in life with the limited identity of a young child, but that is not our essence. We need to identify ourselves as individuals who keep upgrading our thoughts and our self-image.

"I made a firm decision to view myself as someone who is joyful, courageous, kind, and serene. Whenever my thoughts were consistent with this new view of myself, I would tell myself that this was reinforcing this positive identity. Whenever my thoughts were the opposite, I would say, 'This is not who I really am. This is just a thought that I happened to be thinking.'

"I went from seeing myself as a negative person with occasional positive thoughts to considering myself a person who was positive, with once-in-a-while distress-producing thoughts.

"Upgrading my identity had a major impact on my underlying moods. It's like the background music of my life went from a sound track of sadness to a joyful and upbeat sound track. Emotionally I feel like an entirely different person."

Nine-directions mental conditioning: joy, courage, loving-kindness, and serenity

There is a highly effective mental-conditioning technique that will condition your brain to increase feelings of joy, courage, kindness, and serenity.

When your eyes are focused on different directions, various parts of your brain are activated. Focus on these nine directions while repeating the affirmation below.

1. Let your eyes focus on an area that is to the upper left.

Affirm: "Joy. Courage. Love. Serenity."

2. Let your eyes focus on an area ahead of you but higher up.

Affirm: "Joy. Courage. Love. Serenity."

3. Let your eyes focus on an area that is to the upper right.

Affirm: "Joy. Courage. Love. Serenity."

4. Let your eyes focus ahead of you but to the left.

Affirm: "Joy. Courage. Love. Serenity."

5. Let your eyes focus straight ahead.

Affirm: "Joy. Courage. Love. Serenity."

6. Let your eyes focus ahead of you but to the right.

Affirm: "Joy. Courage. Love. Serenity."

7. Let your eyes focus on an area that is lower down and to the left.

Affirm: "Joy. Courage. Love. Serenity."

8. Let your eyes focus on an area that is ahead of you but lower down.

Affirm: "Joy. Courage. Love. Serenity."

9. Let your eyes focus on an area that is lower down and to the right.

Affirm: "Joy. Courage. Love, and Serenity."

I shared this technique with someone who later gave me this feedback:

"I tend to be a bit shy and self-conscious when I enter a room full of people. I went to a few of the rooms where I usually experience this shyness. I mentally practiced this nine-direction technique when the room was empty. I felt as if I was sending out positive energy to all corners of the room. Later, I entered these rooms when other people were there, and I felt much more comfortable than usual. I now associated these rooms with the positive qualities of joy, courage, love, and serenity."

You write your script every time you speak

A head of state knows that what he says is important. So he and his advisers spend time figuring out the best thing for him to say. Professional speechwriters get paid very well for writing speeches for presidents, prime ministers, and heads of companies. Professional scriptwriters get paid large fees for writing scripts for professional actors to perform. Scriptwriters want to successfully write a great script.

Because you write your own script for your everyday life, you can write any script you choose. View yourself as a person who will write life-building scripts.

People who use negative scripts create problematic interactions. People who are frequently angry and stressed out write contemptible scripts for themselves. And so do people who frequently complain and kvetch without accomplishing very much.

Writing your own script before talking means taking a moment to think of what to say. What you say is valuable. What you say has an important effect on the lives of others. So think before you speak. Ask yourself, *What would I like to accomplish for myself and others when I speak?*

The holy Chofetz Chaim used his power of speech to do the greatest good. He consistently avoided causing distress and pain. He mentally wrote his scripts because he knew that what he said would have eternal impact. You would be wise to learn from this model of wisdom and greatness.

Every time you speak, you do so in a present moment. You reveal your character with what you say. Use your ability to speak wisely and kindly.

Several times a day, pay attention to the script you use when you have a dialogue with the most important person in your life: yourself. As you upgrade the quality of your self-talk script, you upgrade every aspect of your life.

> *A student told me that he had heard about another script theory, which prevented him from developing himself the way that he wished he could.*
>
> *In short, he had heard that every person has learned a script, as it were, for his life. He heard that we tend to repeat the patterns of our parents and that we are limited by various things we were told about ourselves. He felt that it is unlikely if not impossible for anyone to improve himself. It would be hard to do and it would take a lot of time.*
>
> *I told him that the Torah concept is contrary to that view. While we are born with a basic temperament, we have a great ability to develop every positive trait that we sincerely desire to develop. We choose what we think, say, and do in each present moment. We are able to begin new habits at any given moment.*
>
> *I kept repeating this point in different ways. I told him about the brain researchers who have proven that new patterns can be started at any time in our lives. I told him that he didn't have to believe me. He should experiment himself*

and see that he can develop the patterns that he wanted to develop.

I told him that there was one condition: He had to practice with the attitude of total belief that he could do it or he would prove to himself that he couldn't. But if he believed wholeheartedly that he could improve, he would.

He saw how certain I was. He put in 100 percent effort. He was tremendously successful.

Use your imagination wisely

Use your imagination wisely. Our Creator has supplied you with a miraculous gift at birth: your brain. It can imagine every possible positive trait, positive quality, positive pattern, and positive way of being.

Unfortunately, some people use their imagination to create needless distress in the forms of worries, fears, and all sorts of excessive stress. They can learn to stop imagining negatively and start imagining themselves the way they want to be.

Use your gift of imagination to build your self-image. See yourself being your ideal self. Replay those images over and over again until it becomes a reality in your brain. Once you know how to do something, your brain reacts to imagination just as it does to external reality. This shows up in modern brain technology.

All skills need practice. You will become more skilled at creating joy, courage, serenity, and love for Hashem and kindness by imagining situations and scenes when you speak and act these ways. More practice eventually will cause these skills to be spontaneous and automatic.

Joyful people create joy with their imagination. People who are not joyful create the opposite. Courageous people create confidence and courage with their imagination. Insecure people do the opposite. Loving and kind people create these traits with their imagination and with their actions. Unloving and unkind people do the opposite. Serene people create serenity with their imagination. Nervous, anxious, worried, and angry people do the opposite.

People who have created many counterproductive mental pictures in the past can decide, "I will use my imagination wisely to the best of my ability from now on."

Repeat with great enthusiasm, "I am committed to use my imagination wisely."

In the beginning, familiar negative imaginings might reappear. No problem! Just choose a new positive mental picture now. Do this calmly and playfully.

Ask yourself, *If I could create any positive quality in my imagination, which quality (or qualities) would I choose right now?*

If you are ever tempted to think that you can't, just imagine that you can!

> *People have told me that imagining a dialogue with their perfect life coach has been highly effective for them.*
>
> *We all have times that we have access to our inner knowledge and wisdom. And we all have times when we speak and act without this wisdom. When you have a dialogue with a wise virtual coach, you gain access to your subconscious wisdom.*

Think of an area where you could benefit from having an inner coach. Mentally visualize what your wise coach would look like. Is he similar to someone you know and greatly respect? The coach could be someone you create who is a composite of the qualities and wisdom of a number of people.

> *Say to your coach, "Inner coach, I need some suggestions about what I might say and do right now," and wait for a response.*

If you find that this works, develop the habit of asking, "What would my wise inner coach say to me right now?"

I can do anything that is not impossible for me to do

We all start off in life as infants without skills. We learned every skill that we now have. Some skills we picked up quite easily. Other skills were difficult, but we were patient and persevered.

As we grow up, it's normal to feel, "I can learn this skill if I really want to," about some skills. But we probably said, "I think that I will never be able to learn this skill, even if I wanted to," about other important skills.

Some things really are impossible for us to do. Everything else is possible. We might need to gain more knowledge to learn how to do it. We might need to melt needless fears that stop us. We might need to have the courage to speak up or take action.

One of the most beneficial attitudes to make your own is: "I can do anything that is not impossible for me to do."

You can decide that this motto will be a guiding force in your life, even if you never thought this way in the past. Believing in yourself this way will enable you to accomplish many goals that you might have considered impossible. People often say, "I can't," when really they can, if they don't let the uncomfortable sensations of fear stop them.

Any fear that you had before this very moment is a fear that you had in the past. The good thing about the past is that it's over. Right now you are in the present. Right now you can imagine yourself saying what you need to say and doing what you need to do to reach the goals that you desire.

Some people are blessed with this "can do" attitude at a young age. I personally wasn't. Even if you feel that you cannot authentically say, "I can do anything that is not impossible for me to do," practice saying it anyway. As you repeat this daily, one day you will finally realize, "It's true. I can do anything that is not impossible for me to do."

> *Someone who attended my recent lecture said to me, "I heard you say that joy, courage, and serenity are skills that we can all learn. But I think that you are wrong. I tried to be happy, but I'm not. I lack courage. And I'm nervous much of the time. I just wasn't gifted with these qualities. I sincerely tried to improve. So either I can't learn these skills or these aren't really skills but natural-born qualities that you either have or don't have."*
>
> *I asked the fellow for his specific attempts to improve. I asked him how much time he actively spent on trying to develop these skills. I asked him which books he read, and how many times he reviewed those books. I asked him which exercises he experimented with, and how much time he spent on them.*
>
> *After a few more questions, it was obvious to both of us that he really didn't do all he could. He didn't read my books on happiness, serenity, courage, and self-talk, or the books by anyone else. He didn't try any exercises. And he didn't consult a coach.*

I told him, "Imagine that you wanted to be an expert at negotiations, at selling, or even at golf, but you didn't read anything on the subject. And you didn't get yourself a knowledgeable teacher or practice effectively. You could say you wished you were an expert, but you couldn't say that you did all that you could before you gave up.

"Right now, write down a plan of some practical things you could do to gain the skills of happiness, courage, and serenity. Then follow through."

"Oheiv es haMakom..." meditation

A wonderful thought to meditate on is taken from the sixth chapter of *Pirkei Avos*. The passage in Hebrew is: "*Oheiv es haMakom, oheiv es habriyos; mesamei'ach es haMakom; mesamei'ach es habriyos.*" This translates to: "Love Hashem, and love people. Bring joy to Hashem, and bring joy to people."

Express gratitude for each breath and allow yourself to breathe slowly and deeply. You can say, "As I continue to breathe slowly and deeply, I express my gratitude for each and every breath."

Then calmly repeat in Hebrew or English, "*Oheiv es haMakom, oheiv es habriyos; mesamei'ach es haMakom; mesamei'ach es habriyos.*" "Love Hashem, and love people. Bring joy to Hashem, and bring joy to people."

Even one minute of repeating this is highly beneficial and elevating. For greater serenity, meditating on this for 10, 15, or 20 minutes is a tool that will help you access a highly serene state.

Some people refrain from meditating because they think, *If I can't do this properly for 20 minutes, it's not worth starting.* But in reality it's a valuable concept to reflect upon, even for short periods of time.

Experiment. Allow your mind to clear, and breathe slowly and deeply. Two five-minute sessions a day for a month will have noticeable effects. If your mind wanders, calmly bring it back to the words you are saying. Continue to reflect on these inspiring words. People who have done so have reported impressive results.

> *Someone told me that his doctor told him that he is suffering from a number of psychosomatic ailments because of the high levels of stress that he regularly experiences.*
>
> *I told him to meditate as mentioned in this section, in addition to anything else he does. Since he had such high levels of stress, he would benefit most if he did this for 20 minutes a session, twice a day.*
>
> *"I know that it would be emotionally and spiritually healthy for me to do this," he said. "And because of my health challenges it would be worth the investment of time. But I'm holding so far away from these lofty ideals that I can't see myself actually doing this."*
>
> *"That's exactly why this would be so beneficial for you," I explained. "In normal circumstances you would probably argue that you can't find the time, and you are too impatient to do this for so long a time. But now you are motivated to do what you can for your health. You will gain so much exactly because you are now far from this way of thinking.*
>
> *"Many people from all walks of life have practiced various forms of slow, deep-breathing meditation. Steady, rhythmic breathing, together with repeating a chant, becomes much easier as you actually do it. You'll find yourself entering a calm, altered state of consciousness and you might be surprised at how much you actually enjoy doing this."*
>
> *He reported that he was highly impressed by how much calmer he was, and people who knew him saw the difference. He was amazed about how his whole relationship with*

the Creator had gained. Moreover, he felt highly inspired to treat other people better than he ever had before. He was motivated to do what was in his power to create more joy for more people.

Lack of self-love causes a deficiency of "love for the Almighty, and love for people"

The spiritual level to strive for is to "Love Hashem (the Creator of the universe) and love people. Bring joy to Hashem, and bring joy to people" (*Pirkei Avos*, Ch. 6). The Torah tells us, "You shall love your fellow as yourself" (*Vayikra* 19:18). That means that we use love of ourselves as a basis for love of others.

People who lack love for their own essence will have challenges when it comes to experiencing authentic love for their Creator and unconditional love for other people. Rabbi Isaac Sher, the Rebbe of Rabbi Avigdor Miller, elaborated on this theme (see *Leket Sichos Mussar*, vol. 3, pp. 49-75).

Your essence is your soul with all of its manifestations. Your body is a vehicle for your soul. When a person says, "I love my self," he is essentially saying he loves his eternal, infinite soul.

The Chofetz Chaim wrote (in *Shmiras Halashon,* Ch. 2): "The Almighty loves each person more than each person loves himself." This means that if we will emulate our Creator, we too will love ourselves. To internalize this concept, say, "Since the Almighty loves me, I love my self."

Some people mistakenly think that authentic love for oneself will cause self-centeredness and selfishness. But the truth is just the opposite. When people have unconditional love for their own essence, they will be kind and generous and compassionate.

A person with authentic love for himself will not have an issue with self-image or self-esteem. When there is love for one's self, there is a profound sense of self-worth. That person's mind and heart will be open to the needs of others.

Individuals who grow up with unconditional self-love will be free from much of the anxiety and nervousness of someone who feels a need to keep proving himself to himself and others.

Fortunate are people who grow up in an environment where the important people in their lives have reached a level of "Love Hashem and love people. Bring joy to Hashem, and bring joy to people." They too will tend to be joyful and loving. Someone who didn't experience this environment must make it a high priority to develop self-love.

It is incumbent upon us to continually strive for character refinement and development. But even before we reach the levels that we strive to reach, it is essential to have unconditional love for our self. This won't make us complacent and lazy. Rather, with unconditional self-love we are more motivated to connect with our Creator and to do His will. We will have the energy and drive to keep developing ourselves with joy and a positive attitude.

The messages about ourselves that we keep repeating to ourselves make an impact on our conscious and subconscious minds. The messages develop healthy self-love. Be willing to repeat frequently, "I unconditionally love my self, even though I am not perfect."

Similar statements to repeat to your self are:

"I love my self even though I have faults and limitations."

"I love my self even though I make mistakes and errors."
"I love my self even though I feel envious."
"I love my self even though I lose my temper."
"I love my self even though I overeat."
"I love my self even though I don't always utilize my time in the best and wisest ways."

When we truly love someone, we care for that person's needs. When we love our self, we strive to meet the spiritual needs of our soul. Therefore, higher levels of love for our true selves will inspire and motivate us to think, speak, and act in ways that meet our highest needs.

> *"My life was a total mess," someone shared with me. "I wasted a tremendous amount of time each day. I felt I had existential anxiety. I was deeply unhappy most of the time. I tried to improve, but nothing I did lasted very long. I felt totally awful about myself. I was greatly criticized as a child. And as I got older, I felt that those criticisms were well deserved. I had a lot of character flaws. To say that I hated myself would not have been an exaggeration. I consulted a number of people but I usually felt worse about myself afterward. They pointed out various ways that I was deficient. They meant well, but I just felt more discouraged.*
>
> *"What helped me tremendously was a kind and warm rabbi who told me, 'You are too hard on yourself.'*
>
> *"'But I'm certain that you would agree that I am an awful person,' I told the rabbi.*
>
> *"'I don't agree that you are an awful person,' he said kindly. 'I do agree that you would be wise to upgrade your thoughts, words, and actions. But your essence is holy and pure. G-d is bestowing life upon you this very moment. If the Creator and Sustainer of the universe believes in you and your potential, so do I. And so should you.'*
>
> *" 'You're just saying that to be kind,' I argued.*
>
> *"'I'm certainly not saying this to be mean,' he said. 'But I am saying this because this is the truth. I see into your heart and soul that you really are a person with high aspirations.*

You kept trying over and over again because your ideals are beautiful and right.'

"'I don't blame you for feeling discouraged. You have a valid reason for feeling this way, based on your history. But your future is not based on that past. It is based on your present awareness. The one major thing that I feel will make a major difference in your life is to begin to love yourself unconditionally,' the rabbi told me.

"'But how can I love who I am now?' I challenged him.

"'Who you are now is really your holy soul. It's the body that gets in the way. Be resolved to love your self totally and unconditionally. You will begin to feel better. When you feel better, you will also feel better about yourself. This will give you greater energy to improve. Optimism about your potential will be a self-fulfilling prophecy. Believe in yourself. I believe in you. Just the way that you are listening to me now shows me how wonderful your essence is.'

"'As you believe in your essence, you will think better. By thinking better, you will also speak and act better. Each small success will keep motivating you to make even more progress.'

"'But always keep in mind that your soul is loved by its Creator. You can't fool the Creator. Even when you try to fool yourself into thinking that you aren't really someone special, you still are. Wake up. You can do great things in your life. You just need to take one small step at a time. Each step will give you more energy to keep going. The Almighty will lead you along the path that you sincerely want to go.'"

The belief of this rabbi began a major transformation in this person's life. Once he was open to the idea that he should love his true self, opportunities opened up. To outsiders it seemed that he became a totally different person. But really he was always a soul that strived high.

"Inner joy" meditation

A great meditation that consists of just two words is extremely effective in increasing the amount of joy one experiences in life. The two words are: "Inner joy!"

Allow your mind to focus completely on the present moment. As you continue to breathe slowly and deeply, mindfully say, "Inner joy!"

Repeat "Inner joy!" as you reflect on how you would feel now if you actually experienced inner joy. See what you would see. Hear what you would hear. And allow yourself to feel how you would feel.

As you keep repeating, "Inner joy," your mind may wander. Calmly keep bringing your focus back to "Inner joy."

As you keep repeating this, recall times when you were joyful. See what you have already seen at previous times when you experienced joy. Allow the feelings of "Inner joy" to spin from your head to your toes. By allowing these feelings to spin and flow, you will be able to extend the inner feelings.

If your mind creates excuses to explain why it might be difficult to be joyful right now, calmly bring it back to the thought of "Inner joy." Let joy enable you to transcend any thoughts and feelings of unjoy.

Imagine how enhanced your life will be when inner joy will be your general way of being. As you visualize this, you will be conditioning your mind for greater joy.

Remember, you only need to create inner joy now, in the present. And the good news is that it's always the present. So you only need to access inner joy when you want a moment of inner joy.

You can transform this meditation into a prayer: "My Father, My King, Creator and Sustainer of the universe, bless me with inner joy." The more frequently you allow the prayer to be answered, the more joy you will experience.

> Someone told me that he was going through a number of challenges. He was basically a happy person but he became overwhelmed when he interacted with critical and verbally aggressive people. He could not avoid a certain individual whose verbal abuse caused him many distressful thoughts and feelings. The actual experiences of negativity didn't actually last long, but he would obsess about them and therefore his experience of distress came up often and lasted a long time.
>
> He had calmly and respectfully asked the person to please refrain, but he didn't get anywhere with him.
>
> Therefore, I first suggested he meditate on the words, "Inner joy." But when I saw that this wasn't strong enough for him, I suggested that he meditate on the words, "Great inner joy."
>
> I told him not to expect this meditation to be effective right away. But if he was patient, with time he would see positive results.
>
> He reflected on this for a while, then he exclaimed, "The greatest inner joy." He surprised me with his level of enthusiasm.
>
> "Whenever your mind wanders to the thoughts and feel-

ings associated with this person, enthusiastically say to yourself, "The greatest inner joy!" I reminded him.

I kept checking up on him. He wished that repeating this would become automatic. I encouraged him to make the effort.

He did and found that it worked wonders for him. Try it and see how it works for you. Be patient and don't give up too soon. For most people, it's always too soon to give up.

The "I radiate joy and love!" Exercise

What is the "I radiate joy and love!" exercise? Enthusiastically repeating, "I radiate joy and love!" of course!

Focus on love for the Creator and love for kindness. Focus on joy for being alive and for all the good that you can do with your life.

Right now, stop reading and repeat as joyfully and enthusiastically as you have ever said anything in your entire life, "I radiate joy and love!"

I recommend starting by repeating this phrase three times a day for two minutes each session. Have fun! Imagine great things happening to you and exclaim, "I radiate joy and love!"

People who got angry easily have found that after repeating this daily for thirty days, they got angry much less easily. People who argued a lot found that if they did this five times a day for two minutes each time, they interacted with much greater harmony.

Before you read on, I would suggest that you spend the next two minutes repeating, "I radiate joy and love!" (You may use a timer.)

If you find yourself in a mood that is the opposite of "joy and love," I would recommend doing the six-minute exercise. That is, repeat, "I radiate joy and love!" for six minutes. If you sincerely want to be in a better mood, repeat this exercise with as much enthusiasm as you can.

After the six minutes, mentally scan your muscles from head to toe and see how much better you feel.

Someone called me and recited a long list of what had already gone wrong with his life. The truth was that he currently faced some challenges, but nothing that was tremendously terrible. He spent an enormous amount of time each and every day in the present rehashing what had gone wrong in the past.

Finally, I interrupted the long-distance caller and said, "Right now I only have a limited time to talk. Let's speak again, but only after you have done the 'I radiate joy and love!' exercise for a week.

"Each time you say this phrase, say it with the greatest excitement and enthusiasm that you can at that moment.

"Keep a log and record the 10 times each day that you repeat, 'I radiate joy and love!' for two minutes each time. It's only 20 minutes total. And you can space it at your convenience.

"No one has to know what is going through your mind. Throughout the day you will find opportunities to do this. Even when your hands are busy, your mind can repeat this exercise."

A week later, he called back to say, "I feel like a brand-new person. Thank you for giving me this precious exercise."

Now that you have read this chapter, you too have this valuable exercise stored in your memory. The more frequently you repeat this exercise, the stronger the neural pathways in your brain become for the statement, "I radiate joy and love!"

Awesome joy

Talmud tells us that each and every person is obligated to say, "The Creator created the universe for me." When fully realized, this awareness will give each of us "awesome joy."

A person who finds a great treasure of jewels washed ashore on a desolate beach will experience great joy. "WOW! I'm fabulously wealthy," he will exclaim.

But this is nothing compared to being the owner and possessor of the entire universe. Our planet has tremendous riches. None of us are the sole user of the planet; we share it with all other human beings. But we can enjoy the sight of every mountain, every park, every tree, and every flower. They are ours to gaze upon and enjoy.

It is very easy to lose touch with this Torah reality of our world. What we physically own, in the sense of having sole rights to use and to sell, is extremely limited. Most of our names do not appear on lists of the richest people on the planet.

But the true definition of wealth is *somei'ach b'chelko* – having joy with your portion. If a person owns a $10 million farm that he recently inherited, but he hates farming and everything associated with it, he is not wealthy. He might have financial assets potentially worth a lot of money, but his lack of joy is the true measure of his wealth. Being unhappy makes him poor in what really counts: emotional wealth.

Awesome joy does not cost money but it necessitates contemplation and reflection to acquire. These thoughts need to be cultivated with intentional focus. The more you focus on it, the deeper this awareness will be integrated and internalized in your mind.

Awesome joy is available to someone who has a daily appreciation of world or of the complexity of his body and brain, eyes and ears, and hands and feet. It may take a lifetime of study to develop this awesome joy, a viewed from the perspective of the classic work *Duties of the Heart* and elaborated on by scholars like Rabbi Avigdor Miller and Rabbi Noah Weinberg.

Even a moment of "awesome joy" opens us up to the possibilities available to us. Study the wonders of the human body. Study the wonders of the natural world here on earth. Reflect on the size and scope of the universe.

Petty thoughts and concerns of the ego can limit our vision. Focusing mainly on trivial pursuits takes our focus from what is tremendously awesome. It robs us of a sublime joy that can be ours.

It would be wise to spend at least a minute a day repeating the words, "Awesome joy." Our Creator is beyond awesome. He is the eternal and infinite. Connect regularly to the awesome potential for the ultimate in joy. It will upgrade the quality of your whole life.

> *"My life is in chaos," someone going through a challenging time said to me. "I can't imagine being joyful. I just want to stop being so totally overwhelmed. The more I try to be happy, the worse I feel."*
>
> *I already knew this fellow. His goal was to get others to acknowledge how awful his life was. He didn't think he could be joyful and he tried to convince others that he was right. The harder one tried to convince him that his*

life wasn't that bad, the more entrenched he became in his argument for the validity of his misery.

"If you keep trying some approach and it doesn't work, doesn't it make sense to try something else?" I asked him.

"I guess so," he lamely replied.

I suggested, "Simply as an experiment, let's try the following exercise. Three times a day for three minutes, repeat the words 'AWESOME JOY!' as enthusiastically as you can. Set a timer.

"Stop repeating to yourself, 'This won't work.' 'This is ridiculous.' 'This is stupid.' 'This is a waste of time.'"

He laughed when I said this. He already knew firsthand that if you believe an exercise won't work, the power of your mind's belief is strong enough to prevent a potentially great tool from working. So I added, "You don't even need to believe that it will work. You just have to give it a real trial.

"In order for this to work, you need to follow through. You have a pattern of giving up too soon. Right now commit yourself to actually do this simple exercise. I know from experience that it works for anyone who does it. When you test it out the way it is meant to be done and a problem arises, we can talk about it and focus on finding a solution. But right now don't argue before you try it.

"Just keep it up for an entire month. It's simple. It's just two words. Again, three times a day for three minutes each, repeat, 'AWESOME JOY!'

"For an experiment to be valid, you need to actually do it according to instructions. The instructions are really simple. Do it with a sense of humor. Have fun. You'll see the amazing impact this has on every aspect of your life.

"You waste so much time each day feeling miserable and then complaining about it to as many people as you can. Spend just nine minutes a day saying, 'Awesome joy.' You have nothing to lose. Please do me a favor and test this out for yourself. No one else can do it for you."

He finally agreed. After a week, with a great look on his

face, he reported, "It's unbelievable how a simple tool as this can be so effective."

Try it out for yourself. Teach it to others. Repeat it with friends, children, or students. The more the merrier. Spread joyful feelings.

Look in a mirror and say to yourself, "awesome joy"

When people complain that they want to feel better, I suggest that every once in a while they look in a mirror and repeat 10 times, "Awesome joy!" As you look in a mirror, you can choose to say anything you want to yourself. People who sincerely wish to increase their level of joy, exclaim, "Awesome joy!"

If you are not in the mood to say, "Awesome joy!" right now, now is when it is in your best interests to say, "Awesome joy!" By the 10th repetition you will not be feeling the way you did when you said, "Awesome joy!" the first time.

The first time you practice saying, "Awesome joy!" in front of a mirror, try to say it when you are already in a good mood. Then you don't need to overcome the feelings of a bad mood. But the sooner you try this out the better, regardless of what mood you are in.

People who have done this at least five times a day for an entire week have reported that it was a lot of fun, and it became easier the more times they practiced.

You can also tell your mirror, "Great courage," "Sublime love for Hashem and kindness," and "Calm inner peace."

> *I was speaking to someone who frequently became angry at his children. He yelled and shouted over minor offenses. His wife was extremely upset at the chaotic atmosphere in the house and insisted that her husband do whatever he could to control his anger.*
>
> *"The fact that you become angry so easily is a sign that you don't have a general feeling of well-being," I said to him.*
>
> *"I sure don't," he replied. "But it's my children's fault. They should listen to me and do what I say. But they tend to dawdle. They are so lazy that it drives me crazy."*
>
> *"There are a lot of approaches that we could try, but I would like to start off with an approach that has nothing to do directly with anger. Rather, we need to find a way that you can create a more pleasant atmosphere in the house."*
>
> *I told him about the benefits of repeating to himself, "Awesome joy!" in front of a mirror a number of times each day.*
>
> *"But that's ridiculous," he angrily said to me. "I'm not even a drop joyful. It's ludicrous for me to say, 'Awesome joy!' as I look at my angry face in a mirror."*
>
> *"You got it!" I said to him. "The look of anger and the look of joy are totally incompatible. Logically, you won't be able to do this. The good thing is that this has nothing to do with logic. It's just creating a new pattern. Since this is so foreign to you, you'll need to do this many times a day. Get yourself a small portable mirror. At least 20 times a day, quietly say 'Awesome joy!' No one has to know what you are saying to yourself.*
>
> *"When you are in better moods, you will be able to communicate with your children in a way that makes them feel better and happier to listen to what you have to say. In the*

beginning don't focus on your children's state. Work on your own. I know this will be difficult for you. But I guarantee that if you are totally determined to do this at least 20 times a day, 10 repetitions each time, you will see favorable results."

It took a long time to convince him that it was worth putting in the small investment of time and effort.

He was surprised by how well this exercise worked. I wasn't.

It's going to become easier and easier for me to...

Consistently telling yourself that something will be easy or difficult brings about that result.

People who say, "Isn't it difficult to be consistently joyful?" make it more difficult to be joyful.

To make it easier to become more joyful, frequently say to yourself, "It's going to be easier and easier for me to be joyful."

Do the same thing to become more courageous or to experience more love for Hashem *Yisbarach*, or to improve any other positive quality. For example, "It's going to become easier and easier for me to make and reach my important goals," or "It's going to become easier and easier for me to be calmer and to think clearly."

Every repetition is stored in your subconscious mind. It's not sufficient to just read this once and then claim, "I know that already." You need the actual experience of repeating it to make it your reality.

A teacher said, "I would like to have a positive influence on my students. I teach them valuable ideas that would have a positive influence on them. But they frequently tell me that it's hard for them to follow through."

"Do you think that it's really too difficult for them?" I asked.

"Not really. I'm not expecting anything unrealistic. But I do feel that if they would be more patient, they would see positive results."

"So in essence you are saying that you personally find it difficult to get your points across to them, is that right?" I clarified.

"I suggest that you keep repeating to yourself, 'I am finding it easier and easier to have the patience to teach them to have the patience to do what is necessary to make the ideas that I am teaching a part of their lives.'"

He liked the suggestion. He repeated this to himself and successfully had a more positive influence on them.

Find the humor

People who find the humor in daily situations frequently enjoy life more than more serious people do.

This reminds me of a story I once thought of. A stern and serious elderly man came to a psychiatrist and said, "I'm nearing the end of my life. I've been totally miserable for many years now. My life has been one big joke."

Upon hearing this, the psychiatrist started laughing hysterically. The perplexed patient started feeling great discomfort.

"Are you making fun of me?" he asked.

"*Chas v'shalom*. I wouldn't do that. It would be bad for business," replied the doctor. "It just struck me as funny that you would claim that your life is one big joke. You look like you haven't laughed in years. If your life is one big joke, you should have found the humor in that big joke of yours."

Only professional humorists have the luxury of having a team of expert joke writers come up with constant new humor. But we can all learn not to take ourselves too seriously.

Never make fun of other people. And don't make fun of yourself. But do find the humor.

And if you can't think of something funny, just laugh. Laughing creates healthy biochemistry.

> *A fellow who was beginning to get involved with shidduchim said to me, "I was told that I need to have a few funny stories to lighten up the conversation. What do you suggest?"*
>
> *"I personally don't have a large repertoire of funny stories," I told him. "But if you want to collect funny stories, keep asking people you encounter, 'What are the three funniest stories you ever heard?'"*
>
> *The fellow laughed and said, "That sounds easy enough."*
>
> *He reported back that on his next date, he found an opportune time to ask this question. It made them both feel great.*

The power of "enough is enough"

Total determination to overcome negative patterns is what influences and inspires people to stop engaging in negative thoughts, words, and actions.

Our thoughts, words, and actions are all based on what we choose in the present moment. Your present thoughts are the only thoughts that you are thinking now. Your present words are the only words that you are saying now. Your present actions are the only actions that you are taking now.

When you think, you have the ability to choose from an extremely large menu of thoughts. When you speak, you choose words and sentences from your past and present vocabulary and ideas. When you take action, you choose an action from all the multitude of actions you could possibly take. Despite the available choices, we easily fall into patterns of habitual thoughts, words, and actions.

When these patterns are negative, counterproductive, and harmful, we need to make a special effort to stop engaging in the negative and begin to choose positive thoughts, words, and actions.

When we decide, "Enough is enough!" we are totally determined to stop the negative and begin the positive. This is how people who make profound changes in their lives do it. At some point they make a passionate decision to get off the negative path and continue their life's journey on the positive path.

It helps to clarify why you so strongly want to end a negative pattern. List the harm caused by the negative pattern. Be clear about how much you will gain from choosing positive patterns.

Stopping negative patterns takes a strong decision on your part. But since you are always in the present when you choose what you will think, say, and do, you only need to make one wise choice at a time.

Remember to focus on the positive action, not on stopping the negative one. Keep your focus on what you *do* want to think. Keep speaking and acting in positive ways. When you think positive thoughts, you are automatically not doing the opposite. When you speak positively, you are automatically not doing the opposite. When you act positively, you are automatically not doing the opposite.

The positive choices become easier to make when you think in terms of long-term joy. When you look back later on, you will have a deeper and more profound appreciation that you had the courage, strength of character, and wisdom to make wise choices.

> *A number of years ago, I had a very gratifying experience with a former student. He had been one of the most negative complainers and blamers that I had ever met. Many things were always irritating and bothering him. He complained a lot about events that had happened many years before. His pity-party lists kept getting longer and longer.*
>
> *Then he moved away and I didn't see him for a long time. When I bumped into him while I was on a trip, I immediately could see the difference in him.*
>
> *"How have things been going for you?" I asked him.*

"You probably remember how miserable I always was," he said. *"I kept up my negative pattern for quite a while. But then one day when I felt my usual unhappy self, I said to myself, 'I can't take this anymore.' Many people had told me that I am causing my misery by myself. I didn't like it when anyone said this, but finally I had to admit they were right. I really wasn't any worse off than many people who considered their lives a source of gratitude and blessing.*

"I remembered times I did feel happy. It was because I focused on what was going right at the time. Even then I could have found things to complain about, but I somehow didn't.

"I said out loud, 'This is totally ridiculous. I'm going to stop being such a whiner. That's it. I will keep finding things that I appreciate and that will be my focus.' After a short while I felt unbelievably better. It wasn't that my life was so much better. It was because I became wiser. I kept gaining a greater realization that it was all up to me all the time.

"I kept hearing positive feedback about my newfound pattern. That kept me motivated to continue thinking and talking about what I liked. Whenever I began to feel bad about the amount of time I wasted complaining and blaming, I told myself that this too was part of the old pattern and I was through with it.

"It gives me a lot of pleasure to be able to share with you how much better off I am. You and others offered a lot of valid, positive advice. But I had to come to the decision on my own. I'm certain that what you and others told me had a cumulative effect. So your time wasn't wasted. Thank you for your efforts."

Don't sell yourself short

Don't sell yourself short. Don't say to yourself in one form or another, *Just who do you think you are?*

You are one of a kind. You are created in the Almighty's image. You are a child of Hashem. You are obligated to say, "The world was created for me." With the Almighty's help, you can do and accomplish any positive thing that you sincerely wish to do and accomplish.

The Almighty gave each and every one of us the amazing power to choose. Every moment we can choose what to think, say, and do. This is the Torah view of you and your potential. Nothing can be higher. Regardless of how many positive things you presently think that you can do, you have the potential to do even more positive things. As you keep gaining more knowledge and keep upgrading your skills, you will become more and more aware of even more positive things that you can do.

Moreover, we are all unique. You are the only person exactly like you who ever was, is, and will be. Only you can do all the positive things that you can do.

Each person has the ability to choose a unique form of greatness. True greatness comes from developing and refining your character to the best of your ability.

Every moment you choose your present thoughts, words, and actions. You have the ability to make great choices.

Ask yourself frequently:

What would be a great thought to think?
What would be a great thing to say?
What would be a great thing to do?

Great choices create a great person. Choose greatness.

A person who is publicity conscious might try to promote himself and become well known. But being world famous or being totally obscure is not relevant to choosing true greatness. True greatness does not need fame and fortune. True greatness is an inner quality.

A person who fails to use his potential will feel frustrated, but a person who consistently chooses true greatness will have an inner feeling of joy. He is fulfilling his mission in this world.

Many people are held back by the thought, *I'm not really a great person. I don't want to fool myself.* But if you needlessly limit yourself, you really are fooling yourself. You are selling yourself short.

Regardless of how you feel, the Creator created you with an inner greatness. Right now make a totally determined decision to create a magnificent life. What specifically would this mean for you? Think, speak, and act in ways that are consistent with a vision of you being all you can be.

At any given moment of your life, you can choose a moment of greatness. Ask yourself a number of times a day, *What would I say and do right now, if I were to choose a moment of greatness?*

> *A father called me up and complained about his teenage son.*
>
> *"I'm ready to give up," he said. "I keep telling my son that he has great potential and it's a shame that he's wasting his life. If he keeps this up, he'll be a failure. I tell him this thousands of times. But he's stubborn. He doesn't change. What*

can I tell him that will get him to stop? I want him to change but nothing I say seems to be helping."

I replied, "There is a basic principle when it comes to trying to motivate and inspire another person. It's obvious when you think about it: 'If what you are doing isn't working, do something else.' If your approach isn't getting the outcome that you were aiming for but it's a message that needs to be heard, then do something different.

"The pattern you are describing just makes your son feel bad. That isn't your goal, is it?"

"Of course not," said the father. "I don't want him to feel bad and he knows it. I just want him to change. I figure that if he feels bad enough about the way he is, he will be motivated to change."

"Perhaps theoretically this might seem like a good idea, but that doesn't mean that it will be helpful. Since you have experimented with this approach over and over again, you yourself have proven that this idea isn't effective."

"I must admit that you're right," said the father. "But what should I do?"

"Give your son an honest vision of the greatness that will be his when he utilizes his G-d-given abilities to create himself in great ways."

"But I don't see him that way," said the father.

"Then that's the very first thing you need to change. The good news is that this change is totally up to you. It's based on the pictures you are seeing in your mind and the self-talk that you choose to say. Even though this will take a leap of faith on your part, you can do it. See your son as he is going to be when he acts the way a great person acts. Show him the respect that you will show him when you are truly proud of how he speaks and acts. Don't just tell him that you will respect him conditionally. Believe in him so much that you actually consider him right now to be the type of person that you are hoping he will become.

"Keep in mind that he is a unique individual. He will never be your robot or your clone. Leave room for his individuality.

"Reinforce his positive actions. Give honest feedback. Before you were berating him for what he was doing wrong. Now you will express your admiration and appreciation for every tiny step of improvement. Remember to do this in a way that he personally finds positive. Don't just say the first thing that comes to your mind. Think carefully. 'What will he feel good about hearing that I can honestly say?' Don't exaggerate. Be real. In the beginning, ignore all of his attempts to test you."

The father successfully changed his approach, and his son began to blossom.

75

Setbacks and disappointments can develop your character

In every life there are moments of setbacks and disappointments. We create our character by the way we handle defeat and failure.

It is in moments of great challenge that we have the greatest opportunity to elevate ourselves, by facing the difficulty with inner strength and courage. The spiritual awareness that the Almighty is with us and gives us the inner resources that we need to prosper and thrive will sustain us when we face adversity.

It can take time until we feel ready to pick ourselves up and go on with our life. At the height of the distressful feelings it can seem that life will never be the same. We might even entertain the thought that we could never be really joyful again. But eventually the pain of the setback subsides. We come back to ourselves. The quality that enables us to grow from our most painful moments is known as resilience. All great people have it and that is what makes them great.

During our moments of great challenge we can pray from the deepest depths of our hearts. These are moments that elevate our soul. We can manifest the greatest love for our Creator. We can become close to Him, and develop an inner greatness that will serve as a great light for the rest of our lives.

During moments of challenge we can inspire ourselves by thinking, speaking, and acting right now in ways that we will feel proud of later on, when we look back at these difficult moments. This can transform the low point of the present into one of our greatest moments.

In such circumstances we won't necessarily experience a moment of joy. But our self-respect and dignity will have grown in ways that they wouldn't have in easier times.

To bring out our best during such moments, ask, "What can I say and do right now that will enable me to grow the most from this entire experience?"

> *I once met someone who had lived a very difficult life. He grew up in poverty and had a number of health challenges. He went through many setbacks and disappointments. At times he was able to improve his financial situation, but his successes never lasted very long. He had reached rock bottom more than once.*
>
> *But when I met him, I couldn't tell how much adversity he had experienced. He looked like a very happy person and he spoke in a very upbeat manner.*
>
> *"With such a rough life, how were you able to keep going?" I asked him. "What is the secret to your resilience?"*
>
> *"Once something is over, it's over," he said to me. "I don't live in the past. I'm like everyone else on the planet; I live my entire life in the present. Yes, I've met people who had it much better than I did, and they keep rehashing the past over and over. They complain and gripe. Early on in life, I*

knew that I didn't want to mentally keep repeating past suffering.

"So I adopted an attitude of, 'Once anything distressful is over, I'm glad it's over.' I want to make the best of the present. I appreciate all that I can appreciate each and every day. When I have food for today, I am grateful for that. I'm not going to waste the great moments of today by moaning about what went wrong before.

"Since I know what it's like to suffer, I am much more compassionate when I encounter the suffering of others. I lack material resources, but I am able to share what I do have with others. My personal joy helps them feel much better.

"When I look back at my life, I think about how I gain spiritually and emotionally in the present from what was challenging about the past. What I went through has given me a deeper sense of meaning in my life. Having an easy life wouldn't have given me what I now have in spiritual abundance. For this, I am eternally grateful. This is the source of my inner happiness."

Envy: the art and science of feeling bad because someone else feels good

Envy prevents you from experiencing joy. When you feel envious of the accomplishments, achievements, possessions, or fame and fortune of anyone else, you personally suffer because of the success of someone else.

If you seek happiness and joy, it's important to realize that those who suffer from envy will be unjoyful and unhappy.

Envy is not usually a conscious choice. A person who is celebrating a joyful occasion will not say to himself, *Why should I bother feeling great for my good fortune right now? I'd rather just focus on the envious thoughts that will ruin the day for me.*

Enviers perceive themselves as helpless victims of their envy. People who are envious often say, "I can't help it. I don't want to feel envious. It just comes naturally and automatically."

"It's not my fault," they might say. "My mind does this to me."

By now you know that you can have greater control over your thoughts and self-talk. You can willfully choose thoughts of gratitude and kindness, thoughts of elevation and spiritual enlightenment.

At the highest level we have the role model of Aaron, the High Priest. He was joyful over the success of his younger brother, Moshe, who was chosen to be the great leader and teacher of the Jewish people. Moshe would save them from slavery and lead them along their journey to the Promised Land.

We would all be wise to emulate this spiritually enlightened soul. Even before we reach this spiritual level, on a purely logical level it makes sense to develop the ability to feel joy for the joy of others. An envious person will always find something to be envious about. Since envy is a source of an absence of happiness and joy, a purely rational person would choose joy over the choice of unhappiness.

Just because something is logical and rational doesn't automatically mean that our brain will make that choice. It is easier to increase your gratitude and joy for all the things in your life that you could be grateful and joyful about. When your mind is full of happiness, there won't be room for the thoughts that create the opposite.

This is a skill like every other skill. It takes much practice to master. But at the beginner's level, it's quite easy. Just ask yourself a number of times each day, *What am I grateful for now?*

People devote a lot of time and effort toward building skills that *might* have a positive payoff. It is 100 percent certain that you will feel great when you successfully master filling your mind with grateful and joyful thoughts. This is a skill that is not dependent on anyone else. You don't need to compete with anyone. Your gratitude and joy is up to you.

It is difficult to overcome strong feelings of envy. But the more difficult it is to do something positive, the greater you become.

Every time you change your focus from envy to joy, you become more skilled at doing this. Regardless of how many times it is necessary, it's worthwhile making the effort. Celebrate progress. Celebrate each success.

> *Someone who used to attend a class I gave on happiness said to me, "When I was growing up, envy was a real challenge for me. I wasn't envious of people whose families had a lot of money and possessions, but I did envy other students who were more successful. I greatly admired and felt good about the successes of students who had humility and didn't show off. But if someone was a boastful show-off, it bothered me on a deep level. I worked on overcoming this fault, but it was a source of great distress.*
>
> *"As I got older I realized how common it was for even very successful people to be envious of others. They have every reason to feel good about their own accomplishments, but they focus a lot of the time on how others were more successful.*
>
> *"I realized that I could only be truly happy if I would overcome this tendency to feel envious. I attended a class where the Rambam's idea of going to the opposite extreme was presented. I made up my mind that I would privately celebrate the successes of people I might feel envious of.*
>
> *"Whether or not I knew someone personally, I began to mentally cheer their successes. Whenever I heard or read about someone being successful, I would say to myself, 'I now allow myself to experience great joy that he is successful.'*
>
> *"In the beginning I just said these words, but I didn't actually feel good. But with repetition it started working. I did this so many times that it became a habit. Eventually I felt good whenever I read about someone's success, even if I didn't formally tell myself to 'experience great joy.' I look back at the development of this skill as a major achievement in my life."*

Choose joy and love to melt anger

The best way to melt anger is to immerse your mind in the present moment with thoughts and feelings of joy, gratitude, kindness, compassion, and love.

Whatever you are angry about already happened. It might have been a short time ago or a long time ago. Right now your emotional state is created by the mental pictures you see now and the thoughts or self-talk you are engaged in now. Your present breathing rate and your posture and facial expression add to your emotional state.

Let's say you were totally motivated right now to be awesomely joyful and totally loving and kind. What self-talk and memories would create feelings of joy? What thoughts about our Father, our King, Creator and Sustainer of the universe would give you feelings of love? How could you use your imagination right now to create joy gratitude, kindness, compassion, and love?

Right now, you can think of the constant kindness of your Creator Who is giving you life this very moment. Tell Him, "I love you." Repeat this a number of times, with more joy in each repetition.

It is amazing how laughter melts anger. A moment of positive laughter creates a positive state. When you laugh, the biochemistry created by your brain is the body's source of good feelings. These chemicals are healthy for you and have healing abilities.

On the other hand, the biochemistry of anger is unhealthy. When you feel angry and would prefer to feel good instead, just laugh. Even if nothing is particularly funny, just laughing will have a positive effect on your immune system.

The more frequently you feel joyful, grateful, and loving, the less frequently you will experience anger. Be resolved to become a more joyful and loving person. When you are joyful and loving, you will be able to speak in ways that put the person you are speaking to in a better state. When you are angry, however, your anger brings out his anger. This creates a negative loop: Your anger causes you both to be at your worst. When you are more joyful and loving you are at your best. This enables you to communicate wisely. This creates a positive loop.

When you are joyful and loving, your creative brain will be able to think more wisely and creatively. You will be better able to think of practical solutions to challenges that arise.

The ultimate solution to anger is not to think about anger, even in the context of managing anger and controlling anger. Instead, think of the positive traits and states that you do want.

As you master patience, you will automatically become angry less often. As you master kindness and compassion, you will be more understanding. This prevents anger.

As you master being centered, focused, and flowing you will be in much calmer states. A calm person stays calm in situations when others become angry.

As you master being joyful and loving, there won't be room in your mind for anger. As you will personally experience, joy and love melt anger, both in yourself and in others.

If you have a challenge with anger, tell yourself, *Right now, I choose unconditional love and awesome joy. I allow all unjoy to melt away.*

Calmly and enthusiastically keep repeating this statement. Notice how positive feelings begin to flow.

> *I met a fellow who had a serious problem with losing his temper. He had gotten into a number of fights and punched a few people. Someone called the police and he was under the supervision of a probation officer. He was told that he needed to attend an anger-management course.*
>
> *He became interested in studying his Jewish heritage, and when he came to a series of classes I was giving, he told me about the court order and added, "Someone told me that you would be a good person to consult because you had written a book called Anger: The Inner Teacher."*
>
> *"I would be happy to discuss transcending anger and overcoming anger," I replied. "But I'm not into anger management. Managing anger is a problematic way of thinking about your goal. Your real goal is to create a more joyful and loving way of being, which includes gratitude, kindness, compassion, and interacting harmoniously with other people.*
>
> *"When you are successful at this, you won't have to worry about anger. Even before you have totally mastered joy and love, just thinking about what you do want will be extremely beneficial."*
>
> *This made sense to him. "I'm certain that this will be acceptable to the probation officer. He seemed fair and sensible. He wants me to succeed."*
>
> *We spoke a number of times about the thoughts and actions that would be helpful in increasing his levels of gratitude, joy, kindness, and harmony with others. We spoke about outcome thinking and about focusing on the wisest ways to achieve what he really wants.*
>
> *The main thing he learned was that it was wiser to focus on the ideals he wanted to integrate rather than focusing on not having the problem. He committed to a lifelong project of character refinement. And so should we all.*

Life is now: creating a moment of... whatever you want to create now

A person who takes a walk of 100 feet and a person who walks 2,000 miles have one major thing in common. They both need to take a first step before they take a second step. Then they need to take a third step and then a fourth. The difference will be how long they keep going. The more steps one takes, the farther one goes.

The same applies when we want to develop any positive pattern. The way you develop any character trait is to take one action and then another and then another. You take one step at a time. And as you keep taking more steps, you end up making those traits and patterns your habitual way of being.

In the exercises that follow you will be reading an entire list of traits to create a moment of each quality. Of course, just a moment of a positive quality isn't sufficient. But it's a start. And starting a tiny step at a time eventually helps a person go a long way.

Don't think about how hard it is to build a trait. Don't talk about how long it takes. Forget about the limiting story of "that's not how I've been before."

In order to experience a positive way of being in the present, you need to choose to think, speak, and act right now in a way that is consistent with that quality. You only need one moment of thinking, speaking, and acting that way to start building up that pattern.

To start a pattern you have a number of options:

1. You might recall a specific time when you already thought, spoke, and acted that way.

2. You might imagine what it would be like in the future to think, speak, and act that way.

3. You might pretend to be able to think, speak, and act that way. Young children do this frequently when they play make-believe. Skilled actors can also do this.

Many adults limit themselves by thinking that they aren't skilled actors. If you do not recall a single time when you had a specific positive quality and you cannot imagine having it in the future, just pretend that you can speak and act this way. Draw upon the skills you built as a child playing make-believe.

Don't limit yourself by falsely claiming that you can't speak and act merely by pretending you can. Just do it! You aren't doing an audition for a star position on a Broadway play. You are doing something better: You are working on developing your character.

As you keep practicing by pretending that you have a positive quality like joy, courage, kindness, or serenity, you will become more skilled at it. I hope you can convince yourself to choose to speak and act that way again.

4. You might find a role model who thinks, speaks, and acts the way you would like to think, speak, and act. Then you can copy the way that role model thinks, speaks, and acts.

Because you can't really know what someone else is thinking, just copy the pattern of the way someone else speaks and acts. Copy the facial expression and body language of someone who really speaks and acts a certain way. When you do this often enough, you will eventually think like someone who speaks and acts that way.

You might want to just condition your mind with thoughts of these traits. Over time you will find that you are speaking and acting in better ways.

This section gives you a list of qualities, traits, and states of ways of being. When you think about creating a moment of a positive way of being, that moment is stored in your brain and is always with you. Every moment adds to the storehouse of similar moments.

You can utilize this list in a way that is best for you at a given moment. First read the entire list. You might want to reflect on just one of these qualities a number of times a day. You might want to select four or five qualities at a time, or however many you need at a given moment. You might want to chant this with a friend or with a group.

You might want to start out with just a moment of a specific quality. Then you can build up to one minute, or five minutes, or even half an hour. That will be awesome!

Every time you read this list, you will, on some level, be increasing the amount of time that your mind focuses on the qualities that you read. These memories are all stored in your portable mental computer, allowing you to access any trait and state that is stored in your brain. This is true even if you only have a moment already stored.

- Life is now, creating a moment of *ahavas Hashem* (love for the Creator).
- Life is now, creating a moment of an alert mind.
- Life is now, creating a moment of appreciation.
- Life is now, creating a moment of asking for what you want.
- Life is now, creating a moment of awakening (*hisorerus*).
- Life is now, creating a moment of awe.
- Life is now, creating a moment of beginning again now.
- Life is now, creating a moment of *bitachon* (trust in the Almighty).
- Life is now, creating a moment of bliss.

- Life is now, creating a moment of bravery.
- Life is now, creating a moment of building inner resources to reach goals.
- Life is now, creating a moment of building your self-image.
- Life is now, creating a moment of calm.
- Life is now, creating a moment of cheerfulness.
- Life is now, creating a moment of *chesed* (kindness).
- Life is now, creating a moment of clear thinking.
- Life is now, creating a moment of compassion.
- Life is now, creating a moment of concentration.
- Life is now, creating a moment of connecting with Hashem *Yisbarach*.
- Life is now, creating a moment of courage.
- Life is now, creating a moment of creativity.
- Life is now, creating a moment of deep thought.
- Life is now, creating a moment of determination.
- Life is now, creating a moment of elevating your self-image.
- Life is now, creating a moment of enjoying this moment just because you are alive and choose to enjoy the moment.
- Life is now, creating a moment of enthusiasm.
- Life is now, creating a moment of fearlessness.
- Life is now, creating a moment of focus.
- Life is now, creating a moment of forgiveness.
- Life is now, creating a moment of friendliness.
- Life is now, creating a moment of fun.
- Life is now, creating a moment of gratitude.
- Life is now, creating a moment of greatness.
- Life is now, creating a moment of happiness. Life is now, creating a moment of harmony (inner harmony and harmony with others).
- Life is now, creating a moment of heartfelt prayer.
- Life is now, creating a moment of high energy.
- Life is now, creating a moment of holiness.
- Life is now, creating a moment of hope.
- Life is now, creating a moment of humility.
- Life is now, creating a moment of humor.
- Life is now, creating a moment of inner calm.

- Life is now, creating a moment of inner peace.
- Life is now, creating a moment of insight.
- Life is now, creating a moment of inspiration.
- Life is now, creating a moment of joy.
- Life is now, creating a moment of joyful self-discipline.
- Life is now, creating a moment of joyful *zrizus* (taking action with alacrity).
- Life is now, creating a moment of kindness.
- Life is now, creating a moment of laughter.
- Life is now, creating a moment of love for Hashem *Yisbarach* ("I love You, Hashem *Yisbarach*").
- Life is now, creating a moment of love for other people.
- Life is now, creating a moment of loving criticism.
- Life is now, creating a moment of mindfulness.
- Life is now, creating a moment of motivation.
- Life is now, creating a moment of optimism.
- Life is now, creating a moment of patience.
- Life is now, creating a moment of persistence.
- Life is now, creating a moment of planning for reaching a goal.
- Life is now, creating a moment of powerful self-mastery.
- Life is now, creating a moment of relaxation.
- Life is now, creating a moment of resilience.
- Life is now, creating a moment of restraint.
- Life is now, creating a moment of seeing the big picture.
- Life is now, creating a moment of self-confidence.
- Life is now, creating a moment of self-reflection.
- Life is now, creating a moment of serene empowerment.
- Life is now, creating a moment of serene patience.
- Life is now, creating a moment of serenity.
- Life is now, creating a moment of silence.
- Life is now, creating a moment of smiling.
- Life is now, creating a moment of spirituality.
- Life is now, creating a moment of *tikun hamidos* (refining character traits).
- Life is now, creating a moment of understanding.
- Life is now, creating a moment of visualizing my most important goals.

- Life is now, creating a moment of visualizing reaching a goal.
- Life is now, creating a moment of vitality and vigor.
- Life is now, creating a moment of wise self-talk.

After reading this list even once, this experience has been added to your mental library. This will upgrade your self-image if you let it. Realize, "I am now a person who has thought about being all the qualities I just thought about."

If someone tells himself, *But I'm not always like that*, that self-talk will limit that person's self-image. Of course, we're not always in any positive state. No regular human being is. But to have a positive trait stored in your brain you only need to have spoken or acted with that positive trait one time.

As you raise the level of your identity, your upgraded self-image will have a positive impact on future thoughts, words, and actions. This will be expressed toward more people in more situations and circumstances.

> *After I taught this exercise to a class, a student commented, "I appreciate this tremendously. I have high ideals and frequently feel a sense of failure that I'm not able to live up to the unrealistic demands I make on myself. When I hear about how I should be, it makes me feel totally discouraged because I remember when I didn't speak or act in ways that are consistent with that ideal. But now that I have a greater awareness that I am always in the present moment, I realize that I only need to think, speak, or act any positive way in just one moment: the present one. This removes a great load off my back. I feel so much lighter."*
>
> *Later on, the student reported that his self-talk improved greatly. Instead of telling himself, "Too bad I'm not always like this," he has developed the habit of telling himself, "I am really glad that I am thinking about speaking and acting this way now. I can see myself speaking and acting this way in real life."*

Abc: spell for joy and upgrading your mind

Joy made easy — just follow the ABC.

A: Appreciate Awesome Aliveness Always.

Almighty is Author of All. Awareness of Almighty's Awesomeness Adds much Awesome Awareness to life.

Appreciative Awareness of All the Almighty gives you now and gave you Already Adds up to An Appreciation Attitude that is Awesome!

Author An Amazing Autobiography, As An Account of Actions and Activities, Achievements and Accomplishments you Aspire to As the Authentic inner you, to Actualize more of your Aspirations.

B: Bless Blissfully. The more Blessings you Bless Blissfully, the more Blissful Blessings you have Blessed, and the more you Bless others, the more Blessed you will be.

Be Beneficially Balanced By Breathing Balancedly.

Bit By Bit Build Brilliant Brain. Building Brain Brings Beautiful Benefits. Build Bridges Between Better and Best to Become Better and Better.

C: Consistently Choose Calm and Centered Clarity and a Cheerful, Caring Consciousness. Choose Calm and Cheerfulness and Congruently Create a Calmer, more Cheerful Character.

Carefully and Creatively Create Courageous Confidence. Can Consult Coach to Clarify. Courage and Confidence Coupled with Compassion and Caring Creates Charming Charisma.

D: Determination and Drive Develop Dynamic Deeds and Divinely Determined Dreams. Don't Delay. Do today!

E: Enthusiasm and Energy Elevate Emotions, Eliciting Enriched Existence.

Every day, in Every way, Exalt the Eternal, the only Enduring Entity.

Essence of Everyone is an aspect of the Eternal.

Each Elevating action you do Elevates you Eternally.

F: Fantastic Fun of Fearless Forgiving Frees Focus and Finds Friends.

Focus Forward for Fabulous Future Full of Finding Favorable Fortunes.

G: Great Gratitude = Great Joy.

Greeting Glowingly Genuinely Generates Joy.

Giant Goals Generate Greatness. Get Going Gladly!

Give Generous charitable Gifts and Greatness Grows.

H: Happiness Helps Heal Humanity. Hopeful Hearts Hear Holy Happiness. Hopeful Hearts Hear other Hearts and Hope to make them Happier. Happier I am, the more Happiness I Happily spread, Helping more Hearts increase Happiness.

I: I am I. I am always I. I am never not I. Inner I Is my authentic Identity. I see myself with my Inner Eye speaking and acting as I Inwardly Ideally want my I to be. Inspirational Ideas Inspire Inner Idealism and are Instrumental In Increasing Intuitive Influence. I

Instantly Inspire my true I when I read or hear Inspirational Ideas. After I am Inspired I am still I, a more Ideal I. Inspired, I aspire to Increase Inspiring others as I Ideally Inspire myself.

J: Joy Journals of Just Joy Jottings generate Joyful Life-Journeys. The more Joy I experience, the more Joyful Jottings I get to Jot in my Joy Journal.

Joyfully Judge favorably and act with Justice. You'll be Judged as You Judge.

K: Kind thoughts lead to Kind words and Kind actions. Each Kind act you do makes you a Kinder person. The Kinder you are, the more others learn from your Kindness to be Kinder themselves. Therefore, your Kind words and Kind deeds make the entire world a Kinder place to live in. You Climb spiritually when you speak and act with Kindness. Kindness and compassion create increased human happiness. You make the recipient of your Kindness happier and you personally become Happier. Even when you can't do all the Kindness that you Kindly want to do, imagine yourself speaking and acting with Kindness to others. As you think of being Kind in your mind, you will find yourself doing more and more actual Kindness.

L: Life Limitlessly Leaves Lessons. Learning Lovingly Lightens Lives. Lost Lessons Limit. Learning Lessons Lessens Limitations. Lists Let Lessons Last Longer. Longer Lasting Lessons create even more Light.

M: Miracle Mind-set Manifests Many Magnificent Moments.
Meaningful Meditations Make Minds More Masterful.

Memorable Memories of Mastermind Meetings Multiply Meaning of My Mission. My Mission is Mine alone. My Meeting My Mission's Message Makes My life More Meaningful and Merry. The more Meaningful My life, the More Magnificent! My Mind keeps this in Mind the More Mindfully I Meditate on what this would Mean to Me.

My Mind is the Maker of the Meaning of all that My Maker Makes part of My Mission. My Mind is up to Me, Meaning I Make Myself the way I Make up My Mind to be Me.

ABC: Spell for Joy and Upgrading Your Mind

N: Now is Now. Now is New. It's Never Not Now. Next Now Not yet Now. Now again it's Now. New Now is Not the Now of before. Next Now becomes the Now of Now and it's also New. It's always Now. I keep getting to experience more New Nows my entire life. That adds a sense of Newness in every New Now. Every Now is an opportunity to make the most of each Now.

Present Now Needs Noticing. Notice Nuances to add knowledge and insight. Now you always know more than previous Nows. Rejoice Now in the Now of the New Now.

O: Observing Objectively Often Opens Our Opportunities. Outcome awareness Of Options Overrides Our impulsivity. Outcome awareness adds wisdom to each potential Outcome.

P: Pray Properly for Persistent Patience and Prosperity, and Perpetual Paradise. Prepare Powerful Positive Personal Programs for Programming Phenomenal Personality. Positive Perspectives Promote Peaceful Perceptions and Positive interactions. Pause for Playful Planning of Purposeful Projects. Plenty of Plans Plentify Potential Possibilities.

Q: Quality Questions and a Quantity of Quality Quotes add Qualitatively to your life.

R: Resilient Renewal Regains Rejuvenation. Rigorously Remove Resistance. Right Road Rightfully Ride. Results Regularly Register.

S: See Superb Self Saying Smart, Sensible Stuff. See Super Self Soaring Spiritually. Selflessly Serve Sincerely. Smartly Sustain Sensational States.

T: Talking Thoughtfully To Thyself and To The other Thoroughly Transforms and Transcends.

U: Understanding Uniqueness Uncovers Unlimited Underdeveloped Ultimate resources and Uncountable assets. Universe is your Divinely given playground to Understand and Utilize in Ultimate ways. Using it wisely is the wisest Use of your time.

V: Vocalization and Visualization Very Verifiable. Visualize

Values Victories. Value your life and Value your time, because you are truly Valuable.

W: We Wander Within Wonderful World Wondering What's next. What do you Want next? Want it to be now. When you Want it to be now, you always get What you Want, because What it is, is always now. I Wonder What Wonderful things you can do When you Wish to be as Wonderful as you can be. When? When it's now. Be as Wise now as you can Wishfully be.

Wisdom Wins Wisely. Wise Willpower Will Win What you Want and Wish for.

Well-being Was Where you Were When you Were an infant. Well-being is What you really Want now. Will Well-being and it Will be Won Whenever you realize that Well-being is What you truly desire as your Way of being.

X: X-factor for "Joy now!"

Y: Yell "Yes" to Your positive possibilities. You can choose to Yell "Yes" many times each day. With each Yelling of "Yes" You keep making a more remarkable You. Yes, it's true, Your personal universe keeps expanding as You expand Your true unique self.

Z: Increase your Zone of joy with joyful *Zrizus*, enthusiastically doing all the good you can. (See *Taking Action* — ArtScroll.)

Allow yourself to be in the Zone of Zest. Pray in the Zone of Zest. Study in the Zone of Zest. Do kindness in the Zone of Zest. The more moments you are in the Zone of Zest each and every day the more Zest you will be adding to your Zestful life.

INSTRUCTIONS:
1. Reread Regularly.
2. Contemplate Carefully.
3. Meditate Mindfully on the Meaning of the Meditations.
4. Now Notice the upgraded New Now. You Never return to ancient Nows since present Nows are always New. Now how do you wish to be Now?
5. You will expand Your universe as You develop Your Self.
6. Deepen Desired Destination. Do Deeds each Day that Develop.

7. Imagined experiences and Insightful Insights Increase your essential I.
8. Joyfully Jot Joyful experiences in your Joy Journal.
9. Heartfelt Happiness Happily Happens. Have many Happy moments as you Happily bring Happiness to more Hearts. Have Happy dreams, and Happier Heightened Higher awareness.

Someone who read this section reported, "The first time I read this, I couldn't really concentrate well on what I was reading. I was feeling very distressed and my mind wandered. It was suggested that I read this again when my mind is in a clearer state. The next time I read this, I thoroughly enjoyed the mental trip that engaged my mind.

"As I read this section each day, I savored various phrases at different times. Throughout the day a number of the messages reverberated in my mind.

"'Life limitlessly leaves messages.' It sure does! Seeing the challenging situations as a life-message helps me remain more objective and open to learn what I can.

"'See super self soaring spiritually.' The pictures that this brought to my mind give me an elevated feeling that even if I'm stuck in a difficulty, I have a super-self part that can find a spiritual solution that my regular way of being wouldn't have thought of.

"I loved the idea of having a 'miracle mind-set.' In the prayers we mention that there are miracles happening each day in our life. I have found that I got used to some of the things that are truly miraculous in my life and I have taken them for granted. When I opened my eyes to the miracles in my life, I saw things that were always there but I wasn't noticing. Noticing them now made me feel unbelievably better.

"'Build bridges between better and best to become better and better.' The idea of 'best' in the sense of perfection is an impossible goal. When I give up the idea that I need to be totally perfect, but I do need to keep getting better, I feel

motivated to keep improving. I can see that this message will keep me on track to keep working on improving myself.

"I have gained immensely from reading this section and I plan to keep rereading it."

A tourist's guide for today on our planet

A wise tourist will clarify the purpose and goal of his trip. We are all just tourists on Earth. Your stay on this planet enables you to store spiritual nourishment for the eternal life of your soul.

Life is a journey that begins the day you are born. Your body's journey on this planet will eventually end, but your eternal soul will live on.

There are two ways to travel on this planet: joyfully or not joyfully. You can choose to raise or lower the spiritual and emotional quality of each segment of each day.

If you choose to be joyful every time you begin to read from this book, that segment of the day will add joyful moments to your life. Those joyful moments are stored in your brain to be accessed at any time. I hope you will decide to continue your journey joyfully, even during the times that you are not reading this book.

Since you are traveling the path of your life regardless of whether or not you experience joy, it makes sense to be joyful for as much of your journey as possible. Choosing joy is beneficial for your Torah study, prayers, and acts of kindness, as well as for your health and well-being. When you are joyful, you get along better with fellow travelers on your life's journey.

The more you realize that choosing to be joyful now is up to you, the more frequently you will decide to choose joy in your present moments.

You can't choose everything in your life, but there are some things that depend totally on you. Other things don't depend totally on you, but your choice of thoughts, words, and actions are up to you. When you choose wisely, you upgrade the spiritual and emotional quality of valuable segments of your life.

To enhance many minutes of your life, ask, "What is the wisest and most spiritually uplifting choice of thoughts, words, or actions right now?"

> Someone challenged me by saying, "I heard you say that choosing joy is up to me. But it's not so easy. I've been through a lot of distress and suffering in my life. I tend to worry and be pessimistic. I can't just change my nature. What do you say to that?"
>
> I calmly replied, "I agree that you can't change your nature. Only our Creator can create a new nature. But I would suggest that what you are calling your 'nature' is really your personal habits. Habits can become second nature. But habits of thoughts are just habits. It does take effort to change a habit.
>
> "As you choose to create joyful moments of gratitude and appreciation in the present, eventually that will become your habitual way of thinking. Then you will eventually feel that it's your nature to be appreciative and grateful."
>
> "But what about my old habits? They won't just disappear," the fellow argued.
>
> "Right now, let's use this conversation to talk about creating a moment of joy. Whatever you say about joy, that is what

you are thinking in the present. You might choose to explain why you are not joyful right now. Or you might choose to explore the possibilities of your being more joyful. Whether you talk about joy or its absence right now, the discussion is still related to joy, isn't it?"

"Yes. But if I think about not being joyful, how will that make me joyful?" he asked.

"It won't. But when you talk about not being joyful, you can choose to think about how wonderful it would be if you could be joyful. And instead of arguing, you could ask me, 'If I were totally determined to be joyful right now, what thoughts could help me?'"

"Okay, so I'll ask you."

"I suggest that you look at yourself as a tourist in life. Let's imagine a tourist who plans to visit 20 cities, one for each day of his trip. When he is in London, he sees the sights and hears the sounds of London. When he is in Paris, he sees the sights and hears the sounds of Paris. And when he is in Jerusalem, he sees the sights and hears the sounds of Jerusalem. When you see yourself as a tourist visiting various places, you realize that what you are seeing and hearing now creates your experience of the present. And this is true for all of us, each moment of each day."

"I see your point."

"So for the next ten minutes let's mentally visit a place we'll call, 'The Garden of Joy, Courage, Love, and Serenity.'

"You create the consciousness you choose with your thoughts. This garden is found exactly where you are at any given moment. A regular tourist needs to travel to different places by walking, riding, flying, sailing, and so forth. But a mental tourist can be in the exact same physical spot as a moment ago, and still choose to be mentally in a totally different place. We can all travel to a place of joy in a split second. Quite amazing, isn't it?

"All you need to tell yourself is, 'I choose joy now. I choose to see joyful sights in my mind right now. I choose to hear joyful words in my mind right now. I allow feelings of joy to *spin and radiate within me right now.'*

"Since it's always now, you can mentally travel to any joyful or serene place, regardless of whether it's real or imaginary," I concluded.

"I can see how this will work for me. I'm willing to try it out," he said.

Are you ready to try it out?

A tale of two towns: what is the difference?

Imagine a visit to two vastly different towns. One town was full of people who felt miserable and treated others in negative ways. The other town was full of people who experienced well-being and joy. They treated others in very positive ways.

In the negative town, the people had a negative view of themselves and were pessimistic about anything becoming better. They evaluated everything that happened in negative ways. They always focused on what they were unhappy about. The complained all the time and constantly blamed others for their unhappiness. They were self-centered and selfish. They felt angry and resentful all the time.

Everything they remembered about the past was negative, and they anticipated negative things happening in the future. They wasted time and didn't have any plans for improving things in their lives. They focused on problems and on what was wrong, with no intention of fixing the issues. They became overwhelmed in the face of the many challenges they faced.

They consistently created negative energy in themselves and in others. They always looked upset and angry. No one ever smiled at others. If they ever saw themselves in a mirror, they just reinforced their own negativity.

But the people of the other town were just the opposite. The people always focused on what they appreciated and were grateful for. They consistently spoke and acted joyfully and kindly. They always found opportunities to help themselves and others. They consistently created meaningful goals. They always assumed that they would benefit and gain from the various situations and circumstances that arose. They focused on potential solutions whenever they thought about a problem.

They kept developing their character whenever they faced a challenge. They saw themselves being the way they wished to be. They consistently accessed positive states whenever they thought about the past. They focused on their inner resources that would enable them to deal intelligently with whatever happened in the future. They always had an authentic smile on their faces when they greeted others. Mirrors always reflected their kind and warm smiles.

What is the difference between the towns? The negative picture describes the inhabitants before you visited that town. The positive picture describes the same town, which was transformed town after you set up "Happiness Clubs" all over the town.

The Happiness Clubs totally changed and upgraded the negative mind-set of the negative people. You were persistent in spreading your kindness and positive attitudes. You brought out a spiritual dimension that was missing before you visited there.

As you personally gain greater mastery over your thoughts and mental images, you will be able to have a positive influence on more people. How? When you are totally determined and dedicated to succeed, you will find ways to help others in real life.

Joy: "it's up to me!"

This section can serve as a summary of the main ideas that will lead to a joyful life.

To help you remember these ideas, the first letter in each sentence spells the principle: "It's up to me."

I create the quality of my life with my ongoing thoughts.
The choice of joy or the opposite is mine.
See, hear, and feel the way joyful people see, hear, and feel.
Unhappiness is created by negative thoughts, words, and actions.
Perspective makes me happy or unhappy.
Talk to myself the way I would if I was a master of joy.
Oneness of humanity gives me many opportunities for kindness.
My unconditional joy and love creates a magnificent life.
Every moment of joy is stored in my awesome brain and I can access those moments whenever I choose.
"It's up to me" now!

"I understand that you do counseling," a fellow said to me. "I have a serious problem. My life is full of great distress. I always worry. And my worrying is driving me crazy."

"You don't mean that literally, do you? You certainly don't seem crazy to me," I replied.

"I guess not. But I feel a lot of distress most of the time."

"It's good that you have decided to do something about your pattern of thinking," I said, "but it seems to me that your biggest problem is one that can be solved right away. It's just the details that need to be worked out."

"What do you mean by that?" he asked.

"You told me that you worry a lot and that this is giving you a lot of distress. Your biggest problem is that you focus on what you don't want, and you are not focusing on what you do want," I explained.

"Isn't that just a minor pattern?" the fellow asked.

"No. It's the heart of your problem. The solution is to keep your focus on what you do want."

"But I do want to overcome my worrying and stop creating so much distress and anxiety."

"I'm a joy coach and self-image builder. When you keep your mind's main focus on what you want, you will automatically not be thinking about what you don't want. Now stop focusing on what you don't want. In the short time that we've been speaking, you've already clarified what you do and do not want.

"You have clarified that you want to stop worrying. That's great. From now on, keep your focus on increasing your moments of joy. Every moment of worry is not a moment of joy, right?" I paused.

"You can say that again."

"And every moment of joy is not a moment of worry, isn't that also right?"

"Now that you mention it, it's certainly correct."

"You have a great imagination. Imagination is a great gift given to humans. People who tend to worry tend to misuse the gift of imagination. They imagine things happening that they don't want.

"Joyful people use their imagination to create positive thoughts about what they do want. Some people see pictures in their minds more clearly than others, but clarity isn't important here. Keep imagining things being the way you would wish them to be. Keep imagining yourself developing the traits, states, and patterns that you want for yourself.

"Imagine yourself experiencing much joy in every bit of progress toward your goals. When you use your gift of imagination the way it could and should be used, you automatically will be free from worry."

He protested, "That sounds almost too good to be true."

"Experiment. Test it out for yourself. Habits of thought can take time to develop. But as soon as you start, you are immediately on the right path. That doesn't take time. It's just a matter of making a decision in the present moment.

"I see from your expression that you feel it would be great if you could actually do this. This decision to use your imagination as a source of joy in your life will totally transform your entire experience of life."

The fellow was sincere about his desire to stop worrying and instead begin living a life of meaningful joy. Once he heard clearly what he needed to do and saw how relatively easy it was, he was determined to choose life-enhancing thoughts. After a short while he felt so much better that he was able to overcome the inevitable ups and downs of life.

Index

A

A calm mind, 184
A drop joyful, 231
A great thought to think, 241
A group of 2-year-olds, 110
A happy and joyful person, 182-3
A head of state, 205
A lot of fun, 231
A magnificent life, 241
A master of joy, 107
A meaningful life, 38
A moment of awesome joy, 227
A moment of greatness, 241
A positive story about yourself, 23
A real trial, 228
A reason to be joyful, 122
A team of experts, 235
A waste of time, 228
Aaron's joy, 248
ABC's for joy, 259-65
Ability to make great choices, 241
Abraham's attribute, 184
Abundance now, 71
Accept that you are a normal human, 178
Accept that you aren't perfect, 178
Accept what you feel now, 39
Access again and again, 197
Access to inner knowledge, 209
Accessing states stored in your brain, 43-4
Accomplish, clarify what, 206
Acknowledge less than ideal, 201
Act and speak with enthusiasm, 44
Act now the way you wish to be, 46
Acting "as if," 107
Activate parts of brain, 203-4
Actors, professional, 205
Adverse situations, 198
Adversity, bounce back, 164
Adversity, face with spiritual awareness, 244

Affirmation, nine directions, 203-4
Affirmation to think of joyful moments, 171
Affirmations for joyful dreams, 154-5
Affirmations for upgrading identity, 200-2
Affirmations, unwillingness to repeat, 198
Aggressive people, 222
Ailments, psychosomatic, 215
Akiva, Rabbi, water on rock, 184
Alert mind, 255
Alignment, self-talk in, 193
Alive, 255
Alive now, 76
All courage is in my mind, 163
All great people have resistance, 245
All is well is a test, 18
All skills need practice, 208
All stress is in your mind, 77
All unjoy melt away, 252
All worry is fear of unhappiness, 175
All you can do, 212
Almighty, love for, 217-20
Almighty loves, 219
Already happened, 18
Altered state of consciousness, 215
Always a soul that strived high, 220
Always breathing in present, 127
Always in the present, 222
Always joyful, 94
Always keep in mind, 220
Always now, 21

Ancient history, 167
Angel, not an, 178
Anger, contemptible script, 205
Anger, melt, 250-2
Angry less easily, 224
Angry people, 209
Answered first, pray for others, 152
Anxiety and self-love, 218
Anxious people, 209
Any positive quality, 209
Any script you choose, 205
Anyone can choose to create more joy, 136
Anything that is not impossible, 211
Appreciate the present, 20
Appreciation, express, 243
Approach, change of, 242-3
Archives of your brain, 21
Arguing a lot, 224
Arguing before trying, 228
Arguing without experimenting, 142
Art and science of envy, 247-9
Art and skill of joy, 86-7
As you believe in your essence, 220
Ask for Divine assistance, 91
Asking for what you want, 255
Association with joy, 204
At a time, one, 238
At best, 183
At my ultimate best state, 44-5
Atmosphere of home, 231
Attitude, beneficial, 211
Attitude of past is over, 198
Attitude of total belief, 207
Authentic inner you, 259

Authentic love for self, 218
Authentic, not, 191-2
Author of all, 259
Autobiography, 19
Automatic habit, 181
Automatic inner joy, 223
Avoid causing distress, 206
Aware of Almighty's existence, 105
Aware of feelings caused by thoughts, 201-2
Aware of your choice of self-talk, 180-1
Awareness, deepen the, 227
Awareness, now, 55
Awesome joy, 226-9
Awful person, 219

B

B.B.B.E.H.H.I.M.P.T., 43
Bad every day, 80
Bad moods, 44
Baharan, Rabbi Avraham, 97
Bake joy cookies, 146-147
Balance, wise, 118
Based on past, not future, 220
Basic temperament, 206
Basis of worry, fear of unhappiness, 175
Be totally in the present with a calm attitude, 167
Before going to sleep, 153
Begin new day any time, 27
Begin new habits, 206
Begin the positive, 238
Begin to feel better, 220
Begin to love yourself unconditionally, 220
Beginning again now, 255

Beginning, in the, 209
Beginning of the day, 152
Being alive, celebrating, 122
Belief, can improve, 207
Belief of the rabbi, 220
Believe in your potential, 219
Believe in yourself, 220
Berate yourself, don't, 150
Best state for now, 42
Best states, 183
Best you, 22
Better feelings in a moment, 39
Better mood, 225
Better than coffee, 176
Big joke, life, 235
Big picture, 18
Biochemistry changes with states, 43
Biochemistry of laughter, 251
Birth, miraculous gift, 208
Birthright to be happy, 177
Bitachon, 176, 255
Bite, joy with each, 148
Bits of progress add up, 194
Bless blissfully, 259
Bless 18 people a day, 151
Bless people with joy, 140
Blessed on the day you were born, 24
Blessing in disguise, 175
Bliss, a moment of, 255
Blocking joyful celebration of life, 123
Blood pressure and states, 43-4
Boastful show-off, 249
Body, vehicle for soul, 217
Body-mind state, positive vs. negative, 42
Book of your life, 36

Index / 277

Book, reading just one time, 185
Book tells you how, 183
Boost of courage, 163
Bounce back, 201
Bounce back from adversity, 164
Brain always with me, 163
Brain, joy created and stored in, 99
Brain, miracle gift, 208
Brain, part of, activated, 203-4
Brain research, joy, 88
Brain stores knowledge, 21
Brain technology, 208
Brainwaves and states, 43-4
Bravery, a moment of, 256
Breakthrough goals, 182
Breath, gratitude for, 28
Breathe as putting down package, 77
Breathe gratefully, 214
Breathing joyfully, 127-9
Breathing style and states, 43-4
Bring a smile to someone's face, 130
Bring joy to people, 214-5
Bring mind back to present, 175
Bring out our best, 245
Brisk walking, 141
Build self-image, 208
Build your identity, 202
Building brain, 260
Building courage, 163
Building Your Self-image, 62, 93, 185
Buttons, fingers as, 186-9
By thinking better, 220

C

Calm, 256
Can be kind and warm, 178
Can do attitude, 212
Can't, I, 212
Care for person's need, 219
Celebrate each moment of joy, 94
Celebrate joyously, 122-3
Celebrate progress, 249
Centered, focused, and flowing, 184
Centered, focused, flowing, 21
Certain in improvement, 207
Challenges develop character, 25
Challenges of life, 19
Change, and *Choose,* 40
Change, I just want him to, 242
Change is up to you, 242
Change of approach, 242-3
Change physiology to change your state, 44
Change, profound, 238
Change the future, 18
Change the past, can't, 18
Chant: joy, courage, love, serenity, 190-2
Chaos, life is in, 227-9
Character, create, 244
Character refinement, 218, 252
Character, reveals your, 206
Charming charisma, 260
Chazon Ish, 105
Checking watch, 128
Cheer success of others, 249
Cheerfulness, a moment of, 256
Chemicals for joy, 96-8
Chesed (Kindness), 256
Child of Hashem, 240
Child playing make-believe, 254
Childhood traumas, 197-9
Children of Creator, 181
Chofetz Chaim, 218

Chofetz Chaim, power of speech, 206
Chofetz Chaim's student, 32
Choice in each present moment, 206
Choice of serenity, 167
Choose joy, decide to, 175
Choose positive thoughts, words, actions, 238
Choose wisely, 22
Choosing power, 240
Chovos Halevovos (Duties of the Hearts), 175
Clapping hands, 129
Clarity, fear of unhappiness, 175
Clarity it can be done, 198
Clear thinking, 256
Clone, not, 243
Clubs, Happiness, 271
Coach, wise inner, 209-10
Coffee, better than, 176
Collect funny stories, 236
Comfortable feeling, 204
Comments of the past, 18
Commitment to upgrade identity, 200
Compassion, 256
Compassionate and kind, 156
Complacent, 218
Complainers, scripts, 205
Complexity of body and brain, 227
Computer programming, 195
Concentration, 52, 56, 256
Condition, one, 207
Conditioning your mind, 195
Confidence and courage, imagination, 209
Congratulations, 28

Connect with Creator, food, 150
Connection with Hashem, a moment of, 256
Conscious awareness of now, 56
Consciousness, forefront of, 190
Consider great actions, 33
Consistently happy, 177
Constant flow of self-talk, 180-1
Constant frustration, 50
Constant mitzvah, love, 183-4
Constantly develop your character, 20
Constructive present moments, 22
Consult coach, 260
Contemplate greatness of today, 34
Contemplate joy, 146
Contemplation, awesome joy, 227
Control over thoughts and self-talk, 248
Controlling one thought at a time, 185
Conversations with Yourself, 185
Cookies, joy, 146
Coping better than imagined, 175
Corners of the room, positive energy, 204
Count joyfully, 125-6
Counterproductive mental pictures, 209
Counterproductive patterns, 238
Counterproductive self-talk, 194-5
Courage, moments of, 162-5
Courage, past, present, future, 196-7
Courageous self-talk, 163
Create character, 244

Create joyful moments, 130
Create positive mind-set, 198
Creating a moment of … 253-8
Creating joy with self-talk, 116
Creating moments of courage, 162-5
Creating moments of kindness, 160-1
Creating moments of serenity, 166-9
Creating more moments of joy, 86-8
Creating needless distress, 208
Creating own life, 198
Creative writing, practicing, 195
Creativity, 256
Creativity, stimulated by walking, 141
Creator believes in you, 219
Creator, can't fool the, 220
Creator's blessing, 25
Creator's image, 181
Critical people, 222

D

Daily habit, 191
Daily habit of blessing people, 151
Day, new, 27
Decide to choose joy, 175
Decide to use imagination wisely, 209
Decision, a passionate, 238
Decision of courage, 163
Deep thought, a moment of, 256
Deepen the awareness, 227
Deepen your understanding, 185
Deeper sense of meaning, 246
Deeply unhappy, 219

Deficient self-love, 217-20
Denying less than ideal, 201
Describe what you do want to do, 29
Dessler, Rabbi E.E., 17
Determination and drive, 260
Determination to be joyful, 119
Determination to overcome, 237-9
Determined, 232
Deuteronomy 10:12, 31
Develop patterns you want, 206-7
Develop your character, 20
Developing from each challenge, 19
Developing positive traits, 182
Developing traits, 87
Devarim, 26:11, 80
Dialogue with yourself, 206
Didn't happen, worry about things that, 175
Diets, 150
Difference, major, in life, 220
Differences in states, 43-4
Different person emotionally, 202
Different person, seemed, 220
Difficult makes you greater, 248
Difficult to be joyful, 233
Difficulty falling asleep, 154
Directions, nine, 203-4
Disappointment and discouragement, 202
Disappointments develop, 244
Disbelief in ability to internalize, 194
Disguise, blessing in, 175
Distress, avoid causing, 206
Distress, creating needless, 208
Distress, from the past, 18
Distress, from worry, 18

Divinely orchestrated tests, 18
Do all you can do for daily joy, 119
Do something else, 142
Do what's right, 164
Do you really want to feel better? 142
Doing all you can, 212
Don't blame you, 220
Don't delay. Do today, 260
Don't sell yourself short, 241
Don't take foolish risks, 176
Doomed, not to be happy, 177
Doomed to constant frustration, 50
Doorway, repeat walking through, 191
Downhearted spirits, reviving, 156-7
Dreams, joyful, 153-4
Drives me crazy, 231
Drop, each, 184
Dropping pens or keys, 143
Dull tone of voice, 139

E

Each breath in present, 127
Each day do something courageous, 164
Each day of our lives, 19
Each drop, 184
Each small success, 220
Earth, stay on, 24
Easier and easier, 223-4
Easier as you do it, 215
Eating wisely, 148-50
Edison and persistence, 113
Effect on lives of others, 206
Effort to stop, 238

Eggs dropping, 144
Ego concerns, petty, 227
Electronic games, practicing, 195
Elephant, pink, 133
Elevate the past now, 73
Elevating your self, 22
E-mails, bless with joy, 140
Embrace down feelings, 40
Emotional lows, 156
Emotional wealth, 227
Emulate our Creator, 218
Emulate spiritually enlightened, 248
Encounter with people, here and now, 64
Encouraging the discouraged, 156
Endorphin factory, 96-8
Energy and drive, 218
Energy and states, 43-4
Energy, sending out positive, 204
Energy sent to brain, heart, 102-4
Energy through imagination, 176
Energy to improve, 220
Enhance many minutes of life, 267
Enhanced emotional life, 176
Enjoy good feelings of imagination, 176
Enjoy sights, 226
Enjoy the good moments, 135
Enjoying meditation, 215
Enough is enough, 237-9
Entering a calm state, 215
Enthusiasm, speak and act with, 44
Enthusiasm, use imagination wisely, 209
Enthusiastically, 224
Entire big picture, 18

Index / 281

Envious and self-love, 219
Environment growing up, 218
Envy, 247-9
Errors and self-love, 218-9
Essence of life, 17-20
Eternal impact, 206
Eternal soul, 22, 218
Eternally grateful, 246
Events, not source of unhappiness, 175
Eventually it will work, 195
Every day bad, 80
Every day in every way, 260
Every moment of joy, 135
Every moment we choose, 240
Every time you speak, 205
Everyone can create a positive mind-set, 199
Everything else is possible, 211-2
Exact nature of each day, 34
Excel in utilizing today, 34
Exceptionally well, imagine all working out, 176
Excessive stress, needless, 208
Excuses not joyful, 222
Exercise of joy walk, 141-2
Exercise, superficial, 198
Existential anxiety, 219
Experience joy, 183
Experience joy for every positive thought, 179
Experiment with meditation, 214-5
Experiment yourself, 206-7
Experimenting, arguing without, 142
Expert at what you practice, 117
Expert in going from bad to good, 35

Experts quoting, 198
Express admiration and appreciation, 243
Expressing frustration, 143
External movements changes states, 44
Eyes focused on different directions, 203-4

F

Facial expressions changes states, 44
Factory, endorphin, 96-8
Faith, leap of, 242
Fallible, accept that, 178
Falling asleep, 129
Fantastic fun, 260
Fantasy, mental, 176
Far from this way of thinking, 215
Fear, key obstacle in life, 162
Fear, uncomfortable, 212
Fearless, 107-8
Fearless forgiving, 260
Fearless, melt fear, 163
Fearlessness, a moment of, 256
Fears, needless, 208
Feel bad, makes son, 242
Feel joy for joy of others, 248
Feel mastery, 194
Feel proud of yourself, 150
Feeling bad about eating, 150
Feeling bad because feels good, 247-9
Feeling bad in present, imagination, 176
Feeling bad you feel bad, 118
Feelings caused by thoughts, 202
Felt worthless and lowly, 178

Fight or flight response, 174
Financial assets, 227
Find people who encourage and inspire, 133
Find the humor, 235-6
Find the time, 215
Fingers, four, technique, 186-9
Five-minute joy walk, 142
Five minutes a day, 191
Flow of thoughts, 180-1
Flowing in best state, 44-5
Focus, a moment of, 256
Focus attention in what you do want, 93-4
Focus attention on now, 52-4
Focus completely on present moment, 221
Focus creates emotional state, 84-5
Focus expands, 20
Focus on the present, 17
Focus on what you do want, 238
Focusing on disappointments, 19
Focusing on wrong and missing, 83
Follow through on plans, 213
Fool the Creator, can't, 220
Foolish risks, 164
Forefront of consciousness, 190
Forgiveness, a moment of, 256
Fortunate, 218
Forward on priority goals, 49-50
Four for Self-creation, 84-5
Four for Self-Creation program, 180-5
Frequent repetition, 194
Friendliness, a moment of, 256
Frustration, doomed to constant, 50
Frustration into joy, 143
Frustration replaced, 20
Fulfilling Almighty's will now, 32
Fun, a lot of, 231
Fun, a moment of, 256
Fun making progress, 193
Fun of success, 149
Fun practicing, 195
Funny, struck me as, 235
Future conditioning, 196-7
Future illusory hopes, 17
Future not based on past, 220

G

Gain clarity, fear of unhappiness, 175
Gam zu l'tovah, 143
Gaze upon, enjoy, 226
General way of being, joy, 222
Genetic makeup, unique, 136
Genius at joy, courage, love for Hashem, kindness, serenity, 192
Get paid large fees, 205
Gift, greatest, 105
Gift, miraculous, 208
Giving up, 194, 213
Glad to realize self-talk, 181
Go beyond fears, 163
Go out of your way to create joy, 130
Goal, imagine reaching, 194
Goal of increasing joy, 94
Goals, 182
Goals, easier to reach, 233-4
Goals, priority, 49
Goals, what stops you, 132
Going for goals, 50
Golf, practicing, 195
Good idea, theoretically, 242

Good mood vs. bad mood, 44
Good news, 222
Good start in life, 24
Grandchildren and joy cookies, 146
Grandchildren inspired, 23
Grateful for each breath, 128
Grateful to the Creator, 184
Gratitude, a moment of, 256
Gratitude on reaching goals, 50
Great choices, 241
Great inner joy, 222
Great people, ups and downs, 201
Great script, write, 205
Great start, get off to, 194
Great things, do, 220
Great tools not working, 228
Greatest day of your life, 33
Greatest gift possible, 105
Greatest good, 206
Greatness, model of, 206
Greatness, unique form of, 241
Grow from each challenge, 37
Guaranteed progress, 195
Guaranteed results, 232
Guide for today, 266-8
Guitar playing, practicing, 195

H

Habit of counting joyfully, 125-6
Habit of joy for others, 249
Habit of thinking wisely, 175
Habit of worry, 175
Habits, begin new, 206
Habitual patterns, 237
Habitually recall joyful moments, 171
Habitually say to yourself, 180-1

Handicap of not remembering past, 18
Happiness Clubs all over town, 271
Happiness, a moment of, 256
Happiness, nine principles, 80-2
Happy times, 239
Hard to improve, 206
Harmful patterns, 238
Harmony, a moment of, 256
Have a joyful day, 139
Having enough for today, 70
Head of state, 205
Health challenge of eating, 149-50
Health, meditation for, 215
Healthy food, 150
Healthy laughing, 236
Hear what you would hear, 221
Heartfelt prayer, a moment of, 256
High aspirations, 219
High performance state, 44-5
High striving, 220
Higher levels of self-love, 219
Highest needs, 219
Highlights each day, 57
Highlights of personal life history, 171
Highly enhanced emotional life, 176
Hilchos Dei'os, traits, 87
History of sadness, 134
Holding you back, emotions, 195
Hole in rock, 184
Holy and pure essence, 219
Holy Chofetz Chaim, 206
Holy soul, who you really are, 220
Honest vision of greatness, 242

Hope, a moment of, 256
Hormones, states, 43
How can I be certain, 177
How do I want to be now? 28
Humble, be, 178
Humility, a moment of, 256
Humor, a moment of, 256
Humor, find the, 235-6

I

I am a victim, 198
I am always I, 260
I am aware, 55
I am resolved to master serenity, 167
I became wiser, 239
I believe in you, 220
I can't, 212
I can't do this, 123
I can't help it, 247-8
I can't just decide to be joyful, 107
I can't take this anymore, 239
I don't blame you, 220
I don't want to fool myself, 241
I feel like a new person, 225
I love my self, even though not perfect, 218
I love You, *Hashem Yisbarach*, 183-4
I radiate joy and love, 224-5
I see, hear, and feel myself, 196
I wasn't able to stop it, 175
I wasn't surprised, 232
I wish you much joy, 140
Ideal self, imagination, 208
Ideal way of being, 46
Ideals remain the same, 201
Identify self, courage, 163
Identity impacts you, 200-2

Identity, key is present, 198
Identity, major role in life, 60-3
If I were a master of joy, 107-9
If it isn't working, do something else, 242
If it's not working, 142
If you don't experiment, 142
Ignore attempts to test, 243
Ignore negative self-talk, 142
Illusory hopes, future, 17
Imaginary limitations, 133
Imagination is not reality, 18
Imagination, use wisely, 208-9
Imagine calm and relaxing place, 77
Imagine great courage, 164
Imagine looking back, 194
Imagine messenger from Creator, 24
Imagine positive traits, 208
Imagining joyful dreams, 154
Immense value and worth, 185
Immune system and states, 43
Impact, eternal, 206
Impatient to meditate, 215
Imperfect, miserable about being, 178
Important, most, in your life, 206
Important traits and states, 183
Impossible, proving, 199
Impossible to always be in ideal state, 183
Impossible, what is and isn't, 211-2
Improve, energy to, 220
Improve the quality of your self-talk, 180-1
Improvement, reinforce, 243
In a joyful state, 183

In the beginning, 209, 243
In the past, present, future, 196-7
Incomplete until reach goal, 50
Infants, all start off as, 211
Infinite soul, 218
Inner calm conducive for clear thinking, 184
Inner changes from external movements, 44
Inner happiness, 246
Inner joy meditation, 221
Inner peace, a moment of, 257
Inner resources, 244
Inner voice and eating, 150
Inner wisdom, access to, 209
Insecure, 164-5
Insecure people, 209
Insight, a moment of, 257
Inspiration, a moment of, 257
Instructions for ABC: spell for joy, 259-64
Intensity, repeating messages, 194-5
Intent to internalize, 190
Intentional focus, 227
Interacting with harmony, 225
Interacting with people, best state, 42
Internalize the awareness, 227
Internalize the concept, 218
Internalized and integrated, 143
Interview people, encouraging, 157
Invest time, worthwhile to, 195
Investment of time and effort, 232
Ironic, desire to be happy causes unhappiness, 175
Isn't it difficult, 233

It's always now, 262
It's up to me, 272

J

Jerusalem Joy club, 82
Jewels, finding, 226
Joy, art and skill, 86-7
Joy Club of Jerusalem, 82
Joy coach and self-image builder, 15
Joy, Courage, Love, Serenity chant, 190-2
Joy for being alive, 224
Joy journal, 130-1
Joy made easy, 80-82, 259
Joy, nine principles, 80-2
Joy, to Hashem and people, 214-5
Joy word, 89-91
Joy workshop for 2-year-olds, 110
Joke, life one big, 235
Journal of joy, 130-1
Joyful all the time, 94
Joyful moments already experienced, 101
Joyful, past, present, future, 196-7
Joyful people create joy, 209
Joyful sound track, 202
Judged as you judge, 261
Just choose a new mental picture, 209
Just imagine you can, 209
Just joy jottings, 261
Just laugh, 236
Just listening, 220
Just makes son feel bad, 242

K

Keep a log and record, 225
Keep climbing, 22

Keep in mind, 220
Kind and compassionate soul, 156
Kind, past, present, future, 196-7
Kindly speak, 206
Kindness, 256
Kindness and compassion for everyone, 184
Kindness, moments of, 160-1
Knew firsthand, 228
Kvetch without accomplishing, 205

L

Label theme of life, 36
Lack of self-love, 217-20
Last breath, 22
Last verse of Psalms, 127
Laugh, 41
Laughing healthy, 236
Laughter, a moment of, 257
Laughter melts anger, 251
Laughter produces endorphins, 97-8
Lazy, 218
Leap of faith, 242
Learn courage from others, 164
Learnable skill, serenity, 169
Learned habit of worry, 175
Learning from others, 200-2
Leket Sichos Mussar, 217
Let go of negative thoughts, 178
Life a total mess, 219
Life coach, 209
Life is for growing, 19
Life is in present, 17
Life journey, choosing wisely, 21-22

Life this very moment, 219
Life-building scripts, 205
Life-transforming personal program, 193-5
Lifetime process of building yourself, 181
Lifetime project, character refinement, 252
Lightbulb and persistence, 113
Limited by script, 206
Limiting story, 254
List the harm, 238
Listening, just, 220
Lists let lessons last longer, 261
Little by little, 183
Live a life of joy, 19
Live one day at a time, 119
Lives of many people, 199
Logical to develop joy for joy of others, 248
Long-term joy, 238
Look in a mirror, 230-1
Looking back at life, 37
Losing temper and self-love, 219
Lot of time to improve, 206
Love, constant mitzvah, 183-4
Love for Almighty, 217-20
Love for Hashem, 28
Love for kindness, 224
Love Hashem, 214-6
Love of self, 217-20
Love others as self, 217
Loves, Almighty, 218
Loving criticism, a moment of, 257
Low self-esteem, 62
Ludicrous to say, 231
Luzzatto, Rabbi Moshe Chaim, states, 44

M

Maimonides, developing traits, 87
Major factors that create your life, 180-5
Major thing, one, 220
Make-believe positive pattern, 254
Makkos 10b, 91, 119
Many types of serenity, 184
Master challenges, 19
Master of joy, 107-109
Master personal program, 194
Masters at feeling bad, 100
Mastery, feel, 194
Mean, not saying to be, 219
Meaning in life, 246
Meaningful each day, 20
Meaningful goals create meaningful life, 182
Meaningful, savor the, 178
Meditation into prayer, 222
Meditation of inner joy, 221
Melt anger, 250-2
Melt needless fear, 211
Melt unnecessary fears, 163
Memories valuable, 18
Mental fantasy, 176
Mental library, added to your, 258
Mentality of victim, 198
Mentally cheer success of others, 249
Mentally elevate past, 73
Mentally picture breakthrough goals, 182
Mentally picture serenity, 167
Mentally scan your muscles, 225
Mentally wrote scripts, 206
Mesilas Yesharim, 18, 44
Message to people with rough pasts, 198
Messages about ourselves, 218
Mezuzah, grateful for breathing, 129
Michtav MeEliyahu, 17
Middle of life's journey, 22
Miller, Rabbi Avigdor, 217, 227
Mind, all stress in 77
Mind, always keep in, 220
Mind has stream of thoughts, 178
Mind-body state, best for now, 183
Mind-body state consistent with thought, 29
Mind-body state, positive vs. negative, 42-5
Mindfully for a month,191
Mindfully say, "Inner joy!" 221
Mindfulness, a moment of, 257
Mind-set, everyone can create, 199
Minyan for counting joyfully, 126
Mirror, awesome joy, 230-1
Misery, validity of, 227-8
Mishlei, 15:15, 80
Mission from Creator, 31
Mission in this world, 182
Mistakes and self-love, 218-9
Mistakes, bounce back, 164
Mitzvah, love is constant, 183-4
Moaning about past, 246
Model of wisdom and greatness, 206
Moments of great challenge, 245
Moments of happiness and joy, 183
Moments of joy, replay, 171
Moments of kindness, 160-1
Mood, better, 225
Mood, miserable, 42

Moods change frequently, 22
Moods, good and bad, 44-5
Most joyful feeling in the world, 105
Most joyful moments, 171
Most valuable skill, 183
Most worries don't become reality, 176
Motivated for health, 215
Motivation, a moment of, 257
Movements, external changes states, 44
Multitude of choices, 37
Muscles, relax, 78
Muscles, scan your, 225
My greatest state, 45
My life is in chaos, 227-9
My Life Until Now, 19
My mind is up to me, 261
My self-image keeps growing, 181

N

Name of traits and states, 28
Names of your positive states, 43-4
Needless distress, 208
Negative patterns, determination, 237-9
Negative person with some positive, 202
Negative possibility in the future, 174
Negative scripts, 205
Negative state, how you are, 42-5
Negative thoughts, 133
Nervous, breathing slowly and deeply, 128
Nervous people, 209

Nervousness and self-love, 218
Neshamah and breathing, 127
Neural pathways, "I radiate joy and love," 225
Neural pathways of brain, 134
Neural pathways to joy, 171
Never think negative thoughts, 177
New goals, 50
New habits begin, 206
News, good, 222
Nine directions, 203-4
Nine principles for happiness 80-2
Nine-word serenity formula, 167
No problem! 209
Non-action, 142
Not in the mood, 230
Not my fault, 248
Not the way brains work, 143
Not thinking of something, 133
Not working, if it's, 142
Nothing practical you can do, 175
Nothing stands in way, 119
Notice joyful moments, 130-1
Notice what is going on around us, 55
Now act the way you wish to be, 46-7
Now, what does the Almighty want, 31

O

Observe objectively now, 55
Obsessing about what might go wrong, 174-6
Obsessing verbal abuse, 222
Obsessions, repeating mental tasks, 152

Index / 289

Oheiv es HaMakom, meditation, 214-5
Once it's over, it's over, 245-6
One attitude away, 19
One big joke, 235
One change of focus, 20
One major thing, 220
One moment at a time, 22
One of a kind, 240
One person, only need, 199
One positive story a day, 23
One small step at a time, 220
One wise choice at a time, 238
Ongoing story of your life, 22
Only happy when reach goal, 50
Only need a present moment of courage, 162
Only you are you, 240-1
Opportunities open up, 220
Opportunity to develop character, 175
Opposite pattern of worriers, 176
Optimism, a moment of, 257
Optimism about potential, 220
Overcome emotions holding you back, 195
Overcoming anger, 252
Overeating, 149-50
Overeating and self-love, 219
Overwhelmed by critical people, 222
Own life, responsibility for creating, 198
Own script, write, 205
Own thoughts cause distress, 175
Owner of universe, 226
Oxygen, grateful for, 28

P

Pain, avoid causing, 206
Pain of setbacks, 244-5
Party, life as, 81
Passing test, 19
Passionate decision, 238
Past, elevate in present, 73
Past only memories, 17
Past shaped our lives, 18
Path we have strong will, 119
Path you sincerely want, 220
Patience of teacher, 234
Patience prevents anger, 251
Patient when enjoy what doing, 113
Patterns of parents, 206
People, feeling positive about, 204
Perfect life coach, 209
Perfect right now, 68
Perform, actors, 205
Performing, best state, 42
Persist, conditioning mind, 154
Persist to master joy, 113
Persistent thoughts and actions, 185
Personal history, unique, 136
Pessimistic about upgrading self-talk, 181
Petty thoughts and concerns, 227
Phone books, 151
Physiology to change states, 44
Piano playing, practicing, 195
Picture, entire big, 18
Pictures of happy occasion, 171
Pink elephant, 133
Pity-party lists, 238
Plan for future, 18
Plan practical things, 213
Planning constructively, 174

Playfully, 209
Playgroup for 2-year-olds, 110
Please refrain, 222
Pleasure of Almighty's awareness, 105
Pleasure passing test, 19
Pleasures of the world, 106
Poem, by Rabbi E.E. Dessler, 17
Point to your head, 100
Poor person, every day bad, 80
Poor in what counts, 227
Portable machine, given by Creator, 186
Portable mirror, 231
Positive, one moment at a time, 37
Positive actions, reinforce, 243
Positive energy, sending out, 204
Positive self-talk, 118
Positive state, how you are, 42-5
Positive stories of you, 23
Positive with some negative, 202
Possible, proving, 199
Posture changes states, 44
Potential, believe in your, 219
Poverty is a test, 18
Power of speech, 206
Power to choose, 240
Practice, all skills need, 208
Practice, time on, 195
Practice positive self-talk, 180-1
Practice to master joy for joy of others, 248
Practicing joyful moments, 101
Pray for joy, 130
Pray for others, 152
Pray for wisdom, 118
Pray with all heart and soul, 52
Prayer from meditation, 222
Prayer to Hashem, 106

Prayer with enthusiasm, 44
Precious, each moment of life, 50
Present awareness and future, 220
Present moment breathing, 127
Present patterns of self-talk, 180
Pretend positive pattern, 254
Prevent problems, 175
Prevents you from accomplishing goals, 132
Principles for happiness, nine, 80-2
Priority goals, 49
Problem isn't thinking negative thoughts, 178
Process of life, 37
Professional speech writers, 205
Profound changes, 238
Program, four for Self-creation, 180-5
Programs to condition your mind, 196-7
Progress, bits of, 194
Progress in short time, 94
Proud of son, 242
Proverbs 15:15, 80
Proving oneself, 218
Proving possible, 199
Psalms, last verse, 127
Psychosomatic ailments, 215
Publicity conscious, 241
Pushing "save" button, 128

Q

Qualities born with, 212
Question for now, 32
Quiet of the night, 154
Quitting prevents goals, 113
Quoting experts, 198

R

Rabbi's belief, 220
Rambam, developing traits, 87
Rational to choose joy for joy of others, 248
Ratzon, a strong will, 119
Reach important goals, 233-4
Reading a book just one time, 185
Ready to give up, 241-2
Real about feelings, 172
Reality in your brain, 208
Reality is now, 17
Really your holy soul, 220
Reason to be joyful, 122
Recall times you were joyful, 221
Refinement of character, 218
Reflect on inner joy, 221
Reflection, awesome joy, 227
Refrain from speaking negatively, 164
Regrets about past, 22
Rehashing what went wrong, 225
Reinforce positive actions, 243
Reinforcement is necessary, 197
Rejoice with all the good, 80
Relationship with Creator, 215-6
Relaxation, a moment of, 257
Releasing stress, 76
Relive joyful moments, 99
Remember times felt happy, 239
Repeat joyfully, 197
Repeating patterns of parents, 206
Repeating things, 194-5
Replay joyful moments, 171
Replay positive images, 208
Resilience, 245
Resilience, a moment of, 257
Resistance, no, 2-year-olds, 111

Resolve to improve self-talk, 180
Respecting conditionally, 242
Responsibility for creating own life, 198
Responsible for the world, 181
Rest of life begins again, 27
Reveal your character, 206
Review this book, 114
Reviving downhearted spirits, 156-9
Richest people, 226-7
Ridiculous, 194
Ridiculous, this is, 228
Right now I am alive, 123
Right now I am aware, 55
Right to retain victim status, 198
Robot or clone, not, 243
Role model, view self as, 198
Role model of positive patterns, 254
Role models, learn from, 200-1
Rough past, 198

S

Sadness sound track, 202
Salty food, 149
Savor each kindness, 161
Savor the positive, 178
Say, "Inner joy!" mindfully, 221
Saying to be kind, 219
Scan your muscles, 225
Script, writing own, 205
Script theory, 206
See, hear, and feel joy, 196
See what you would see, 221
See your ideal self, 208
Seeing the big picture, 257
Self-centeredness, 218
Self-confidence, a moment of, 257

Self-conscious, affirmation to overcome, 203-4
Self-control, joy of, 149
Self-Creation program, 180-5
Self-development, lifelong project, 184
Self-development program, 180-5
Self-discipline, joy in, 149
Self-doubt, moments of, 156
Self-esteem, 218
Self-esteem, low, 62
Self-fulfilling prophecy, 220
Self-image, 22
Self-image, keep upgrading, 202
Self-image, past and present, 60-3
Self-image and mood, 44-5
Self-image keeps growing, 181
Self-image of success, 149
Selfishness, 218
Self-love, 217-20
Self-mastery, a moment of, 257
Self-produced chemicals, 96-8
Self-reflection, a moment of, 257
Self-talk, constant flow, 180-1
Self-talk, wise, 118
Self-talk of joy, 116-8
Self-talk refers to all the thoughts we think, 185
Self-worth, 218
Send joyful energy to brain, heart, 102-4
Serene empowerment, a moment of, 257
Serene patience, a moment of, 257
Serene *zrizus*, 184
Serenity, creating moments of, 166-9
Serenity walks, 168
Setbacks, 244

Share with other humans, 226
Sher, Rabbi Isaac, 217
Shidduchim, 236
Shmiras Halashon, 218
Short stories each day, 36-38
Shy, nine-direction affirmation, 203-4
Shy and joy, 137
Simple exercise, 228
Sincerely want path, 220
Situations and scenes, imagine, 208
Six-minute exercise, 225
Size and scope of the universe, 227
Skill of joy for joy of others, 248
Skill of positive states, 182-3
Skills need practice, 208
Slow, deep-breathing mediation, 215
Smart to be in control, 176
Smiles produce endorphins, 97
Solution, anger, 251
Son, approach with, 242-3
Son, makes feel bad, 242
Soul, identify with, 22
Soul, our essence, 49
Soul enveloped in sanctity, 105
Soul is your essence, 217
Soul on a mission, 31
Sound track of my life, 202
Source of good feelings, eating, 149
Speak, every time you, 205-7
Speak and act better, 220
Speak and act with enthusiasm, 44
Speaking in present moment, 206
Special, really, 220

Speechwriters, 205
Spin inner joy, 221
Spirits, reviving downhearted, 156-9
Spiritual goals, 49-50
Spiritual needs of our soul, 219
Spiritual practices with enthusiasm, 44
Spiritual thoughts, 178
Spread joyful feelings, 229
Standards, unreachable, 178
Start, get off to great, 194
Start at any time, 206
Start imagining wisely, 208
Starting a pattern, 254
State, head of, 205
States fluctuate, 27
States of joy, courage, kindness, serenity, 196
States, B.B.B.E.H.H.I.M.P.T., 43
States, moment-by-moment experiences, 183
Status of victim, 198
Step, one at a time, 220
Stop imagining negatively, 208
Stop stopping yourself, 47
Stopped by fear, 212
Stops you, what, 132
Store in your brain, 197
Stories stored in brain, 21
Story of our life, 36
Story of your life, 22
Stress, needless, 208
Stress, releasing, 76
Stress and meditation, 215-6
Stressed-out, scripts, 205
Strive for more, 179
Strongly want to end, 238
Struck me as funny, 235

Study, concentrate during, 52
Stupid, this is, 228
Stupid to needlessly cause self pain, 176
Subconscious messages, 218
Sublime joy, 227
Success, each small, 220
Success of others, cheer, 249
Success of younger brother, 248
Success takes as long as it does, 134
Successful at times, 149
Successfully improved, 207
Suffering from envy, 247
Suffering from self-talk, 194-5
Suffering made spiritual, 198
Sufficient repetitions, 198
Superficial exercise, 198
Superhuman, not, 178
Surprised at meditation, 215
Surprised it worked, 232
Sustainer of universe believes in you, 219
Sweet food, 149
Symbol of victory, 150

T

Take a joy walk, 141-2
Take a moment to think, 206
Taking Action, 185
Take ourselves seriously, 235
Tale of two towns, 270-1
Talmud tells us, 226
Task at hand, 55
Teacher's patience, 234
Technology, brain, 208
Temper and self-love, 219
Temperament, basic, 206
Ten-minute tryout, 194-5

Tennis, practicing, 195
Tension, releasing, 76
Test, prepared for, 19
Test it out, 228
Test taking and joy, 97
Test the nine principles, 81
Tests, life is 17
Thank you for your efforts, 239
The greatest inner joy, 222
Theme for living, 69
Theoretically a good idea, 242
Theory, script, 206
They were right, 239
Think carefully, 243
Think how you want to be, 29
Think of your past, think joy, 170
Think, speak, and act courageously, 183
Think what to say, 206
Think wisely about past, present, future, 175
Thinking elevates you, 33
This too is for the good, 143
This won't work, 228
This won't work for me, 198
Thoughtless comments, 18
Thoughts about past can stop us, 46-7
Thoughts always in the present, 185
Thoughts easily wander, 55
Thoughts of courage, 163
Three funniest stories, 236
Thumb, left and right, 186-9
Tikkun hamidos (refining character traits), 257
Time, lot of, to improve, 206
Time not wasted, 239
Times you were joyful, recall, 221

Today, greatest day, 33
Today, having enough for, 70
Today a new day, 27
Today first day, 194
Toddlers, teaching joy to, 110
Tone of voice, 139
Too soon to give up, 223
Tools won't work if…, 228
Torah concept of choice, 206
Torah concept of who we are, 181
Torah verse for gratitude, 80
Tourist's guide for today, 266-9
Train your brain, 144
Traits, developing, 87
Traits, patterns of thoughts, feelings, words, actions, 182
Traits have names, 28
Tranquility, a test, 18
Transcend unjoy, 222
Transcending anger, 252
Transform frustration into joy, 143
Transform today, 35
Transformation, major, 220
Trauma, childhood, 197-9
Treat other people better, 216
Tried my hardest, 178-9
Trivial pursuits, 227
True greatness, 241
Truly love, 219
Trust in Hashem, 176
Trust in the Almighty, 255
Truth, saying because of, 219
Try something else, 227-8
Trying, arguing before, 228
Trying over and over again, 219-20
Two five-minute sessions a day, 215

Two-minute exercise, 224
Two-year-olds, 110

U

Ultimate best state, 44-5
Ultimately for my good, 176
Unbelievable how it works, 229
Uncomfortable sensation of fear, 212
Unconditional love, 217
Unconditional self-love, 218
Under your control, 175
Understanding, deepen your, 185
Unfamiliar at first, 194
Unfortunate use of imagination, 208
Unhappiness, basis of worry, 175
Unhappiness, don't choose, 248
Unhappiness, not using mind right, 88
Unhappiness in future, 174
Unhappy childhood, 117-8
Unique, we are all, 240
Unique life mission, 31
Unique to you, your moments of joy, 136
Universe created for me, 226
Universe was created for him, 181
Unjoyful, from envy, 247
Unjoyful people, 209
Unkind, 209
Unloving, 209
Unnecessary fear, in mind, 164
Unreachable standards, 178
Unwillingness to repeat, 198
Upbeat self-talk, 118
Upgrade every aspect of your life, 206

Upgrade self-talk, upgrade life, 117
Upgrade serenity, 167
Upgrade what you say to yourself, 180
Upgrading story of your life, 37
Upgrading your identity, 200-2
Ups and downs, 201
Use imagination wisely, 208-9
Use speech wisely, 206
Use your mind wisely, 175
Using negative scripts, 205
Utilize gift of life, 27

V

Validity of misery, 227-8
Valuable, what you say is, 206
Valuable skills, most, 183
Value and worth, immense, 185
Vayikra 19:18, 217
Vehicle for soul, 217
Verbally aggressive people, 222
Verse for gratitude, 80
Vibrantly alive, 42
Victimhood, 197-9
Victims of envy, 247
View today as greatest day, 33
View yourself, 181, 205
Vision of being all you can, 241
Visualize being joyful, 222
Visualize how much gain, 192
Vitality and vigor, a moment of, 257

W

Wachtfogel, Rabbi Nosson, 40
Wake up, 220
Walk, determination to, 120
Walk, take a joy, 141

Wander, calmly bring back mind, 221
Wanders, if mind, 215
Wasting his life, 241-2
Wasting time and self-love, 219
Wasting time on distress imagination, 176
Watch, checking, 128
Water, drinking, and serenity, 168
Water, dripping on rock, 184
Way of being, joy, 222
Ways of being, 254-8
We are all unique, 240
Wealth, true definition, 227
Wealth is a test, 18
Weinberg, Rabbi Noah, 227
Welcome to this planet, 24
Well, all is, a test, 18
Well, imagine working out, 176
Well-being, 231
Well-being, state of, 184
What am I being asked now?, 31
What am I grateful for now?, 248
What had gone wrong in past, 225
What might go wrong in future, 174-5
What would be best for me now, 42
What would I like to think and feel now? 39
What would inner coach say, 209-10
What you say is valuable, 206
What's wrong and missing, 83
When thinking of past, think joy, 170-3
Whiner, stop being, 239
Who do you think you are? 240
Wholehearted belief can improve, 207
Will of Almighty, 32
Willfully choose gratitude, 248
Willing to try new pattern, 143
Wimpy identity, 165
Wisdom, access to inner, 209
Wisdom, aware of future results, 18
Wisdom, model of, 206
Wisdom today, 34
Wise balance, 118
Wise inner coach, 209-10
Wise risks, 164
Wise thoughts, one at a time, 22
Wise to upgrade thoughts, words, actions, 219
Wish to be, act the way, 46-7
With each and every step, 141
Wonderful essence, 220
Wonderful time, 194
Wonderful traits, 196
Wonders of the human body, 227
Word that creates joy, 89-92
Work on your own state, 230-2
Working, if it's not, 142
Works for anyone who does it, 228
Workshop on joy for 2-year-olds, 110
World created for me, 240
World created for your benefit, 24
World famous, 241
Worries, needless, 208
Worry, 18
Worry, obsessing, 174
Worse, feeling, 194-5
Worth, immense value and, 185
Worthwhile to invest time, 195
Write a great script, 205

Write down joyful moments, 130-1
Write own script, 205
Writing speeches, 205

Y

Yell "Yes" to your positive possibilities, 263
YES, JOY!!! 144
Your holy soul, who you really are, 220

Z

Zone, in the, 44-5
Zone of joy and zest, 263

This volume is part of
THE ARTSCROLL SERIES®
an ongoing project of
translations, commentaries and expositions
on Scripture, Mishnah, Talmud, Halachah,
liturgy, history, the classic Rabbinic writings,
biographies and thought.

For a brochure of current publications
visit your local Hebrew bookseller
or contact the publisher:

Mesorah Publications, ltd

4401 Second Avenue
Brooklyn, New York 11232
(718) 921-9000
www.artscroll.com